THE COTSWOLDS
TOP TEN

C000111490

This little book is a condensed version of Goldeneye's Cotswold Guidebook. Goldeneye have been publishing Cotswold Travel Guides in various formats for 35-years and this is the second time a Top 10 has been identified by us. The Top 10 chosen in each category has not been done lightly and it may well be that these are not to everyone's taste. In an Age when time is at a premium and when the traveller seeks only the best and is given to short breaks it seems an apposite moment to re-publish this book. Those chosen are included on merit, and merit alone. We gain no advertising revenue from them for appearing in this book. We do, however, welcome your feedback.

What and where is the region known as the Cotswolds? To those who know it, this may seem like a silly question. However, it is a place that manifests itself in many different ways to different people. Even down to the area they would define as the Cotswolds on a map. To some fashionistas, and magazine editors, the Cotswolds runs comparison to the New York Hamptons and Tuscany. Whilst to others the name is synonymous with wool and hunting, stone walls and majestic churches. From my point of view and for the purposes of this book, the area stretches from Chipping Campden in the north to Bath in the south, and from Gloucester to Woodstock, west to east. Given the restriction on space, only the town of Bath, and Bath Abbey are described – for to give Bath its full measure, it deserves a book in itself.

The Cotswolds derives its name from two Saxon words: 'Cote' - sheep fold, and 'Wold' - bare hill. This references the importance of sheep in the development of the area. And, it is to the Cotswold Lion sheep that one must look to for the origin of wealth and endeavour that brought prosperity to this region.

The Cotswolds region is perched on the central section of a ridge of oolitic limestone. The geological structure has thus had a profound and lasting affect on the landscape, and 'look' of the area. The oolitic limestone that forms these hills has the appearance of 1,000s of tiny balls, like fish roe and is between 200 and 175 million years old.

This ridge has been tilted on its side and is run off with streams and river valleys that lead off in a south-easterly direction to feed the Thames basin. On the western edge the scarp is steep in places with outcrops of rounded hills, notably Cam Long Down and Bredon Hill and makes for fine walking country and pleasing views across to the Malvern Hills and Wales.

Neolithic Man found refuge on these hills from the swamps of the Severn and Thames flood plains. The Celtic Dobunni tribe established hill forts where they farmed, bartered their crafts and founded coinage before the Romans arrived. They were not a warlike tribe like their neighbours the Silurians (Welsh) and eased into a compatible relationship with the conquering Romans to build *Corinium Dobunnorum* (Cirencester) into the second largest Roman settlement in Britain with a populace of 12,000 inhabitants.

The Saxon farmer laid the foundations of prosperity for the medieval wool merchants and it was these merchants who built the great 'Wool' churches and the great manor houses.

More latterly, the Cotswolds have come to represent elegance and wealth. In the C18, Bath and Cheltenham epitomised the elegance, hedonism and splendour of the Georgian era.

The landscape is rich in imagery: dry-stone walls divide the vast, sweeping sheep pastures and lazy, winding, trout streams meander through the rich pastureland. And, scattered across this landscape you will come across quaint hamlets undisturbed by coach, sightseer or time itself. All this makes for an idyllic scene rarely bettered in England.

In recent times this region's close proximity to London has attracted wealthy residents and an increase in second homes bought by out-of-towners. This brings with it all the associated benefits and disadvantages. The region also attracts glitzy minor celebrities with their hangers on in tow and the seemingly necessary trumpet and fanfare. This has opened the flood gates of more high-class restaurants and dining pubs which is a benefit to all (who can afford them).

Pulteney Bridge, Bath

Bath. Bath will captivate you today as it has done so down the centuries, from the Romans to Jane Austen, to Robert Southey and the Romantic Poets, to the Rugby aficionados jostling to get into the Recreation Ground. There is surely only one way to see Bath (apart from the top of an open double-decker bus, or from a hot-air balloon) and that is to walk. The Bath springs were discovered by the mythical King Bladud in 863 BC, King of the Britons. The Celts venerated the site but it was the Romans in about 60-70 AD who developed the hot springs and built a wall around the 23 acre site naming it Aquae Sulis. The site held warm to hot, to very cold baths, sweating rooms, massage areas and fitness rooms. It prospered for 400 years until the Romans withdrew from Britain in 410 AD. In 973 the Abbey was chosen as the setting for the coronation of King Edgar and in 1157 it received the seat of a Bishopric. The city saw much prosperity in the Middle Ages due to the sale of Cotswold wool. But, the heyday of Bath began over a 40-year period when three men of immense vision transformed the city from 3,000 into the Georgian city of 30,000 citizens. They were Beau Nash, John Wood, and Ralph Allen. Today, Bath is an educational centre and hosts many festivals.

A bustling shopping centre with many independent retailers. There appears to be a café or bar on every corner. For those arriving by car best to leave it at Park-and-Ride near the Race Course at Lansdown on the northern side of the City or purchase hourly tickets from most shops. Beware of bus lanes. Food & Drink: Green Bird Café, Noya's Kitchen, Dark Horse, Woods, Bell Inn, Star Inn. (86/D8)
visitbath.co.uk

Bourton-On-The-Water. Described as 'The Venice of the Cotswolds' for the River Windrush is spanned with low graceful bridges. It is the most visited village in the Cotswolds but one that invites mixed opinions. It can be charming on a quiet, frostbitten morning but is best avoided on a busy bank holiday. You must look beyond the crowds and wander the little streets for there are some beautiful houses to admire. Bourton may not thrill the jaded teenager or hard-bitten traveller but it will delight small children. Bourton has its fair share of pubs that cater for the tourist. Perhaps the most traditional bar is in the Old New Inn undergoing refurbishment. Tearooms are plentiful. July Carnival. Water Game - August bank holiday. Food & Drink: Bakery On The Water, Dial House Hotel. (99/K8)

Broadway. 'The Painted Lady of the Cotswolds' is a term often used to describe this village. The honey-coloured stone captivates the visitor today as it did in the C19 when William Morris and his pre-Raphaelite friends settled here. A slow walk up the High Street will unfold some large and impressive houses that have been homes to Edward Elgar, JM Barrie (Peter Pan), Ralph Vaughan Williams and Laura Ashley. These great houses with bow windows, dormers and finely graduated stone roofs are usually hidden behind statuesque gates. It has its fair share of hotels, restaurants, tearooms and art galleries. Food & Drink: Broadway Deli, Crown & Trumpet Inn, Lygon Arms, Russell's, Market Pie. (104/F9)

Burford. The first major Cotswold town you come to if travelling from the east and what an Introduction. The wide High Street with its classical Gables atop gracious houses slopes down to the dreamy River Windrush. Once an important coach and wool centre bursting with activity, hostelries and dens of rumbustious entertainment. A history of civil rights and religious tolerance prevailed here with the Burford Levellers. On 17 May 1649, three soldiers were executed in Burford Churchyard on the orders of Oliver Cromwell. These three had sought to undermine the authority of Cromwell whom they considered to be a dictator, rather than a liberator. This event is celebrated every year with song, dance and speeches. Today, there are any number of inns and pretty cottages hidden down the side streets. The churchyard is a quiet spot with decorated table tombs. Feast of the Dragon and Street Fair in June. Food & Drink: Mrs Bumble, The Priory, The Angel, Lamb Inn, Lynwood Café. (94/B3)

Cheltenham. A smaller version of Bath, often described as 'the most complete Regency town in England'. Elegant Regency buildings overlook the crescents, squares, tree-lined avenues and spacious parks. Cheltenham remains, in historic terms, a young town of a mere 300-years. It grew as a spa after George III had approved the waters in 1788. Thereafter, distinguished visitors such as George Handel and Samuel Johnson came to be revitalised. The Promenade is one of the most attractive shopping streets in England which becomes progressively more independent and up-market as you trudge with heavy bags and depleted purse west towards Montpelier.

Broadway High Street

MAIN CENTRES

Style and fashion epitomise this smart town. Youth and hedonism, a-plenty. Cheltenham is proud of its calendar of festivals but it is during the Cheltenham Festival of National Hunt Racing which takes place in March that the town takes on a carnival atmosphere. A centre of administration, commerce, education, high-tech industries and secret surveillance. The Countryside Commission and UCAS have their headquarters here. It is a most congenial town that could well be described as the centre for the Cotswolds. Its motto is: Salubritas et Eruditio 'Health and Education'. If you can achieve either of these then your luck is in. Food & Drink: Curry Corner, Koj, Le Champignon Sauvage, The Retreat, Suffolk Kitchen, Crazy Eights. (101/L7)

Chipping Campden. If you chose to visit just one Cotswold village make sure it's this one. There is no better introduction. The harmony of Cotswold stone mirrors the town's prosperity in the Middle Ages. The Gabled Market Hall was built in 1627 by the wealthy landowner Sir Baptist Hicks whose mansion was burnt down in the Civil War and the remains are the two lodges beside the Church. The Church of St James is a tall and statuesque 'Wool' church. William Grevel, one of the wealthiest wool merchants is remembered in the church on a brass transcription which reads: 'the flower of the wool merchants of all England'. Opposite Grevel's House is the Woolstaplers Hall, the meeting place for the fleece (staple) merchants. Dovers Cotswold Olympick Games & Scuttlebrook Wake, June. Food & Drink: Campden Coffee Co., Huxleys, Volunteer, Cotswold House Hotel. (105/K8)

Cirencester. One of the finest and most affluent towns in the Cotswolds lies surrounded by a plethora of attractive villages whose populace (often second home owners) tend to shop and hobnob in Ciren (as the locals call it). The smart shops and bars reflect the riches of its patrons. As the Roman town *Corinium*, it became the second largest Roman town (after London) in Britain. Its strategic position at the confluence of the major routes (the Fosse Way, Ermin Way and Akeman Street) combined with the vast rolling sheep pastures brought great wealth in the Middle Ages. The history of Cirencester and the Cotswolds is well documented at the impressive Corinium Museum. On the outskirts of the town stands the Royal Agricultural University, famous for producing generations of estate managers and farmers from all classes of society. All the best eating places appear to be on Black Jack Street. Monday and Friday are market days. July Carnival. Food & Drink: Made By Bob, Jack's Coffee Shop, Organic Farm Shop. (92/B8)

Moreton-In-Marsh. Perhaps the first Cotswold town you'll visit if coming from the north and along the ancient Fosse Way. And, what an impressive spectacle. The wide main street built by the Abbot of Westminster in 1220 for the sheep and arable sales is today a lively scene on market day, every Tuesday since King Charles I granted the town a Charter in 1637. But its origins go back to the Romans who built a military camp around 43-50 AD whilst planning the construction of the Fosse Way. It remains the largest town in the Central Wolds and is dominated by the Market Hall built in 1887 by Lord Redesdale, father of the Mitford sisters. Look out for the Curfew

Tower, an unusual phenomenon on the corner of Oxford Street dated 1633 which rang until 1860. A fine centre given to a number of inns, art galleries and independent retailers. Associated with the English Civil War, for the Royalist Cavalry was based here. Moreton (Agricultural & Horse) Show - 1st Saturday in September. Food & Drink: Cacao, Mrs T Potts, Tilleys. (99/L2)

Stow-On-The-Wold. With a name like this it is bound to attract visitors and it has and does so to this day for with its exposed position at the intersection of eight roads (one being the Fosse Way) Stow has been party to some momentous events in history. The Romans used Stow as an encampment and route centre. The Viking merchants traded down the Fosse Way, but it was the Saxon hill farmers who laid the foundations for the fleece which created wealth for the wool merchants who used the great Market Place for sheep sales of 20,000 or more. It still has free parking and you may wander freely about and admire the art galleries and the antique shops. More recently, the hostelries have been renovated and small hotels revitalized. For Stow has become a centre of Cotswold hospitality, again. But, wrap up before you climb that hill. 'Where the wind blows cold' so the song goes. Food & Drink: Cotswold Baguettes, Le Patissier Anglais, Kings Arms, Old Butchers. (97/L5)

Stroud. Stroud is not your typical pretty Cotswold town. It was as close to the dirt of the Industrial Revolution as any other town in the Gloucestershire Cotswolds with few architectural gems. Its attraction lies in its energy and artistic ambitions. There has been a liberal, bohemian attitude at play here since the group of Tolstoyan Anarchists settled at Whiteways in 1898. There is a lively community of writers and artists living in the surrounding valleys. A busy café culture pervades, too. The weaving industry all began in a couple of cottages up the hill in Bisley (Jilly Cooper's domain), This moved into the town where 150 mills were soon in action using the water-powered valleys. But, as the C19 progressed much of this cloth-making moved north to the West Riding of Yorkshire. The surrounding valleys provide wonderful walks through combes and woodland that are so very different from the Central Wolds. Look out for the Subscription Rooms built around 1833. Fringe Festival - 2nd week of September. Arts Festival - October. Food & Drink: Mills Café, The Diner, Jrool Bistro. (90/F6)

Market Hall, Chipping Campden

SMALLER CENTRES

Bliss Tweed Mill, Chipping Norton

Chipping Norton. A well situated hill-top town affording spectacular views over the surrounding countryside. Mentioned in the Domesday Book. The new Market Place was built in 1205 and is today surrounded by elegant houses with Georgian facades. But it was the wool industry established in the C13 that brought wealth to this corner of Oxfordshire and like so many before them and after, the wealthy merchants invested their coppers in the C15 'Wool' church in order to guarantee a place in heaven. The town's attraction is that it is very much a small market town responding to the demands of the local populace and is little affected by Cotswold tourism. It is home to some celebrities: Jeremy Clarkson, David Cameron and until his death, Ronnie Barker, who ran an antique emporium. Bookshop with coffee shop. Mop Fair in September. Food & Drink: Jaffe & Neal. (96/E5)

Evesham. An attractive market town with tree-planted walks and lawns beside the River Avon. Centre for the Vale of Evesham's fruit growing industries. Abbey remains. Simon de Montfort, who fell at the Battle of Evesham in 1265 is buried in the churchyard. Almonry Heritage Museum. (104/B6)

Malmesbury. Claims to be the oldest borough in England (although Barnstaple in North Devon may dispute this) - established in 880 AD. Military strategists have described its hilltop location as the best naturally defended inland position of all ancient settlements. No wonder then that King Athelstan, the first King of all England, chose it as his home. Set on the edge of the Cotswold escarpment, it is a cheaper place to stay than the more central towns. Its spirit though lies with the Wiltshire landscape. Dysons, the innovative design company of electrical goods is the major employer and has brought some much needed zest, style and money to this isolated town. However, James Dyson was not the first inventor to work in the town. You must go back to the free-spirited monk, Eilmer, in the C11, who designed and built his own hang glider (see Malmesbury Abbey). Food & Drink: Old Bell. (89/K6)

Nailsworth. In the last few years this little town has come alive! Transformed into a thriving, bustling shopping centre with bakery, restaurants, tearooms, arts and craft shops. An eclectic mix of Cotswold domestic and industrial architecture is to be seen dotted about the hillside overlooking a wooded valley. Its position is convenient as a centre for visiting Bath and the south Cotswolds.

Food & Drink: William's Food Hall, Wild Garlic, Hobbs House, Olive Tree. (90/E9)

Northleach. An attractive Cotswold village noted for its church and Market Place. Often overlooked because the A40 now bypasses the village which at first left it out on a limb. The village elders have done much to restore the lifeblood of this little community. It is worth a journey for the 'Wool' church, buildings and museum. Food & Drink: Wheatsheaf Inn, Ox House, Black Cat Café. (92/F2)

Tetbury. A market town with a fine church, St. Mary's. The town's recent claim to fame has been due to its proximity to Highgrove, Prince Charles' home at Doughton. The opening of his Highgrove shop on the High Street has brought a flux of visitors to the town with coaches bringing the traffic to a standstill. How this helps the rest of the town's merchants, one can only guess. Today, it is the Cotswold's centre for antiques. It has also had much welcome investment in the shape of new shops, galleries and places to eat and drink. The Woolsack Races on May Bank Holiday are fun to watch and cause great merriment if you are not forced to carry the heavy woolsack. Those with weak backs (or common sense) are best left to be onlookers. Food & Drink: Quayles, Close Hotel. (89/G3)

Tewkesbury. One of England's finest Medieval towns set at the confluence of the rivers Avon and Severn. Just look up at the gables of the many ancient buildings and admire (or venture into) one of the 30 narrow alleyways that make up this historic place so magnificently brought to life in *John Moore's Brensham Trilogy*. In the Middle Ages Tewkesbury was a flourishing centre of commerce: flour milling, mustard, brewing, malting and shipping. Today, it has its flourmills and is a centre for boating and tourism. It is still a busy market town of half-timbered buildings, overhanging upper storeys and carved doorways. Note the new Tourist Information Centre and Out of the Hat Museum which symbolize the ambitions of this town. Food & Drink: 1471 Deli. (101/H2)

Winchcombe. This small town lies cradled in the Isbourne Valley. It was an ancient Saxon burh (small holding) and famous medieval centre visited from far and wide for the market, horse fair and monastery which was destroyed in the C16. You can still walk the narrow streets beside the C16 and C18 cottages but do look up and admire the many fine gables above the shop fronts. There's a local saying: *Were you born in Winchcombe?* which is directed at those of us who leave doors open. It can be a wee bit drafty. For those who visit Sudeley Castle give yourself some time to explore here. Food & Drink: Food Fanatics, 5 North St., Lion Inn, Wesley House. (98/B4)

Witney. The largest shopping centre in West Oxfordshire, and a dormitory town to Oxford that has seen rapid expansion in the last 20-years. A town of hustle and bustle with a good share of attractive limestone buildings. Note the C17 Butter Cross with gabled roof, clock turret and sundial, the Town Hall with room overhanging a piazza and across Church Green the unusually handsome spire to the Parish Church, visible from far and wide. Witney has a fair compliment of ancient hostelries and the Angel Inn overlooking Church Green is steeped in history. Ethnic restaurants are plentiful

SMALLER CENTRES

Old Flour Mill, Tewkesbury

and diverse in their culinary arts. There have been signs of Iron Age and Roman settlements but the first records of any activity date from 969 AD. The Bishop of Westminster built a palace in 1044 which was eventually excavated in 1984. In 1277 the town's business centred on the fulling and cloth mills. In the Middle Ages gloves, blankets and brewing were the staple industries. Earlys of Witney, the blanket makers were in business for 300 years until quite recently. All of this has been ably recorded in the Blanket Hall and Cogges Manor Countryside Museum. Food & Drink: Angel Inn, Blanket Hall, The Fleece. (94/F4)

Woodstock. A pretty town of stone built houses, interesting shops and smart hotels and a practical centre for exploring the eastern Cotswolds and Oxford. Famous for glove-making in the C16 and for Blenheim Palace (great walks), the birthplace of Sir Winston Churchill (1874-1965) who is buried in nearby Bladon churchyard. There area number of antique shops, art galleries and a fascinating museum plus a melee of delis, inns, restaurants and coffee shops. Food & Drink: Woodstock Arms, Hampers, Chef Imperial, Feathers Hotel. (97/L10)

You May Also Like to Consider:

Wotton-Under-Edge. As the name suggests, Wotton hangs on the southern edge of the Cotswold escarpment. In its long history the Berkeley family have dominated the town with varying success. King John's mercenaries devastated the Berkeley's property in the C11. Later, the simmering dispute between the de Lisles and the Berkeleys was sorted out in the latter's favour at the Battle at Nibley Green in 1470. The Berkeleys were generous patrons; Katherine Lady Berkeley established one of the country's first grammar schools here in 1384. Weaving and cloth making grew from cottage industries in the C13. Wotton is a quiet market town with some splendid C17 and C18 buildings. The countryside (The Bottoms) to the north of the town is quite outstanding, and popular with walkers. Isaac Pitman, 1813-97, who invented shorthand lived on Orchard Street. The Ram Inn is probably the town's oldest building, but it is to St Mary the Virgin that all historians will be drawn. Food & Drink: Ram Inn. (88/A4)

Bibury. Described by William Morris as one of the prettiest villages in England and few would argue with him. It attracts the crowds and is thus the stop-off point for many coach tours. It is a honey-pot village made up of rose-covered cottages set behind idyllic kitchen gardens, and all overlook the sleepy River Coln inhabited by swans, trout and duckling. During the C17 Bibury was notorious as a buccaneering centre for gambling and horse racing. Food & Drink: Trout Farm, Swan Hotel, William Morris Tea Rooms. (93/G5))

Castle Combe. Is this a soulless Hollywood film set once visited by thousands of Japanese and US tourists or is it one of the prettiest villages in the south Cotswolds lieing sheltered in a hidden valley surrounded by steep, wooded hills? Given the recent demise of American and Japanese coach parties, the post office and gift shops have closed. It is a museum piece more recently used for the film *War Horse*. In former times, an important medieval, wool centre evidenced by the weavers and clothiers' cottages that descend from the Market Cross to By Brook and the three-arch bridge. There is parking at the top and bottom end of the village. Food & Drink: Castle Inn, White Hart. (87/H2) castle-combe.com

Duntisbournes, The. A group of isolated hamlets dotted along a beautiful wooded valley. Duntisbourne Abbot stands at the head of the valley. The Dunt Brook flows through each hamlet. The road to Duntisbourne Leer runs adjacent to the stream. Middle Duntisbourne and Duntisbourne Rouse are two farming hamlets, the latter famous for its idyllic Saxon Church. (891/L5)

Eastleach. The twin hamlets of Eastleach Turville and Eastleach Martin face each other across the River Leach. The ancient clapper bridge (Keble's Bridge) connects the two and was built by the Keble family whose descendant John Keble was curate here in 1815. He founded the Oxford Movement and is know for his volume of religious verse *The Christian Year*. In spring, hundreds of daffodils grow on both banks and hidden behind the trees is the Norman Church of St Michael and St Martin. Across the river the tiny church of St Andrews. Food & Drink: Victoria Inn. (93/L6)

Snowshill

Great Tew

Great Tew. A sensationally beautiful village lined with ironstone cottages covered in thatch and stone tiles. Much of the village was designed by the Scottish architect, John Claudius London. The Falkland Arms is named after Lord Falkland who lived here, and who died fighting for Charles I at the Battle of Newbury. Food & Drink: Falkland Arms, Baxters Café. (97/J4)

Guiting Power. A hidden, somnolent estate village that surprisingly manages to support two pubs, a village shop and bakery, a nursery school and an active village hall. The blue-grey cottages belong to the Cochrane Estate (or Guiting Manor Amenity Trust) that has thankfully saved this village from greedy developers and second homers. The Church of St Michael & All Angels lies on the edge of the village and has some Norman features, a beautiful Tympanum and some weather-beaten tombstones. It was an early Anglo-Saxon settlement called Gyting Broc. A classical and jazz music festival is held in late July for the past 38-years and attracts many artists of international renown. Food & Drink: Old Post Office, Hollow Bottom, Farmers Arms. (98/E6) guitingfestival.org

Naunton. A pretty village surrounded by rolling sheep pastures and overlooked by some steep gallops. The handsome Church has some interesting gargoyles and a stone pulpit. Food & Drink: Black Horse. (99/G6)

Painswick. Its local description as '*The Queen of the Cotswolds*' is justified. The houses and cottages are built from a grey, almost white limestone in marked contrast to Broadway and Chipping Campden and some of the buildings have a Palladian, statuesque dignity about them. Look out for the Court House and The Painswick (hotel). Wander down the pretty side streets and visit the churchyard famous for the legendary 99 yew trees. The 100th yew tree has been planted time and again but has never survived. Painswick is one of the gems of the south Cotswolds and is a worthy base from which to explore this region.

Lower Slaughter

It is also connected to a network of footpaths including the Cotswold Way so you can arrive by car or taxi and then just walk for the rest of your stay. Food & Drink: Pooch Coffee House, The Painswick, St Michael's Restaurant, Falcon Inn, Rococo Garden. (90/F4)

Slaughters, The. Lower Slaughter is one of the most popular villages in the Cotswolds. Little bridges cross the Eye Stream which runs beside rows of golden cottages. The much painted C19 redbrick Corn Mill stands on the western edge of the village. Upper Slaughter is a couple of miles upstream and has an old Manor House once lived in by the Slaughter family, an old Post Office with a beautiful kitchen garden and along a lane past the church, a ford crosses the stream hidden beneath lush greenery. Food & Drink: The Old Mill, Slaughter Country Inn, Lower Slaughter Manor and Lords of the Manor Hotel. (99/J7)

Stanton & Stanway. A charming village with houses of warm honey-coloured stone restored by Sir Philip Scott, 1903-37. Centre for equine excellence in the Vine, a popular horse riding centre. The Mount Inn is a welcome refuge if one's tackling the Cotswold Way. Stanway is dominated by the outstanding Manor House. In its grounds one of the country's finest tithe barns designed with the Golden Proportion in mind and across the road a thatched cricket pavilion set on staddle stones. The beautiful Gatehouse is C17 and was probably built by Timothy Strong of Little Barrington. It bears the arms of the Tracy family. The little Church of St Peter has C14 origins and some amusing gargoyles. Food & Drink: Mount Inn. (98/D1/2)

You May Also Like to Consider:

Bisley, Coln Dennis, Coln Rogers, Coln St Aldwyns, Frampton-On-Severn, Minster Lovell, Sapperton, Sheepscombe, Sherborne, Slad, The Ampneys, The Barringtons, The Swells, The Wychwoods...to name but a few.

CAFÉS/DELIS

Bakery On The Water, Bourton-On-The -Water. Located just past the bridge, opposite the Cotswold Motoring Museum. An established business for 85-years run by the 4th generation, and now 5-years in Bourton. An artisan bakery, serving a simple breakfast (no fry ups), homemade cakes and bread - all made on the premises. 01451 822748 (99/J8) bakeryonthewater.co.uk

Broadway Deli, 16 High St., Broadway. You can't miss it, with a Fiat 500 in the window, fruits and veg outside and once inside you will salivate at the cakes, pastries and pies. Open for breakfast at 8-11.30, lunch 12-4.30. 01386 853040 (104/F9) broadwaydeli.co.uk

Broadway Tower, Morris & Brown. This is a new Eating Out and shopping experience. The old barn has been re-branded and converted into a posh, top-notch café-restaurant with flagstone floors, log fires and quality gifts. Open daily. 01386 852390 (104/F10) morrisandbrown.co.uk

Cacao Bean, High St., Moreton-In-Marsh. For those of you fortunate to have experienced delicious cakes whilst travelling in Austria and Germany you are in luck. iHerewith a pleasure to behold. A coffee, pastry and cake shop. 01608 652060 (99/L2) cacaobean.co.uk

Campden Coffee Company, Harts Silversmiths, Chipping Campden. A rustic café with a reputation for superb coffee, cakes and sarnis. Open M-F 9-4.30, W/Es 10-4.30. 01386 849251 (105/H8) campdencoffeecompany.co.uk

Jack's Coffee Shop, Black Jack St., Cirencester. Serves the best coffee (according to my Octavian spies), and amazing homemade cakes. You can sit, al fresco. Further up the street is Jesses Bistro, Butchers in the Cotswolds for many generations, so, if they can't get their meat right, what hope is there for the rest of us? The fresh fish trawls in from Newlyn. Open for lunch, M-Sa and dinner, W-Sa. 01285 641497 (92/B8) jessesbistro.co.uk

Jolly Nice Farm Shop & Café, Frampton Mansell. Rarely have I tasted a more scrumptious burger! Ice cream parlour, farm shop and butchery. Plants for sale. Eat out or in. Open daily 8-7. (91/J8) harrietsjollynice.co.uk

Le Patissier Anglais, Stow ss

Williams Food Hall, Nailsworth ss

Le Patissier Anglais, The Square, Stow-On-The-Wold. Herewith, a delectable experience for those with a passion for pastries, home-made mousses, savoy quiches and coffee. No bread. The Proprietor is a Chocolatier who trained with Albert Roux. So, if you seek a personal service and to chat with a Maestro. Open M-Sa 9-5, Su 9-1. When he sells out, he closes. 01451 870571 (99/K5) lepatissieranglais.co.uk

Made By Bob, Corn Hall, Cirencester. A food emporium open from 7.30 for breakfast, lunch and afternoon teas. It's got Ciren's Ladies of Means in a frenzy of excitement, all rushing in for their champagne cocktails and made-up TV dinners. 01285 641818 (92/B8) foodmadebybob.com

Mrs Bumble, 31 Lower High St., Burford. A Lancashire lass who knows, and loves her food. It is where I always stop for a baguette, and a deli to prepare for a walker's picnic. Try her olives, sumptuous cheeses, scotch eggs and pastas. Open 8.30-5.30. (94/B3)

You May Also Like to Consider:

William's Food Hall & Oyster Bar, 3 Fountain St.,Nailsworth. In need of a lunch time sandwich or seafood (delivery Thursdays) to take home and bake. This deli has been spoiling the locals for so long they have probably forgotten how lucky they are. Restaurant opens for breakfast and coffee. Open daily. 01453 832240 (90/E9) williamsfoodhall.co.uk.

Seymour House, Chipping Campden

PUB-GRUB & ALES

Bell at Sapperton. Popular dining pub decorated with natural stone walls and polished flagstone floors where winter log fires provide a comfortable ambience. Local beers. Al fresco dining in summer. 01285 760298 (91/K7) foodatthebell.co.uk

Fox Inn, Lower Oddington. Origins are C11 with flagstone floors, open fireplaces and wooden beams. Wholesome 'gourmet' style, pub grub. 01451 870555 (99/M5) foxinn.net

Golden Heart, Birdlip. A centuries-old coaching inn serving a range of local ales and food from sandwiches to good pub-grub. Garden with pastoral views. 01242 870261 91/K2) thegoldenheart.co.uk

Mount Inn, Stanton. One of the most spectacularly located inns affording views across to the Malverns and Welsh Hills. A valued stop-over if walking the Cotswold Way. Donnington ales to assuage a mighty thirst, and wholesome pub grub. Popular on summer evenings, so book. 01386 584316 (98/D1) themountinn.co.uk

Plough Inn, Ford. The decor is traditional; flagstone floors, settles and olde-world charm. Cosy and popular with the horse racing set and good-value nosh. Not a bad place to seek advice for the 3.30 at Cheltenham or Hereford. 01386 584215 (98/E4) theploughinnatford.co.uk

Seven Tuns, Chedworth. This wonderful ancient inn has had tempestuous times. Sometimes open, then closed. Hopefully its future is secured. Always a hostelry to find a comfy corner to prepare oneself for long evenings of vivid conversation, dominoes and the bountiful pints of golden ale to be succoured after standing on the green sward of Chedworth's Cricket field. Live music and quiz nights. 01285 720630 (92/C3) seventuns.co.uk

The Fox, Great Barrington. What a pleasure that this pub with rooms has not been plagued by over zealous interior designers who are brain-dead when it comes to understanding the necessities of the Great British Pub. It has remained the same for years, thankfully. The old settles and tables, log fires and ambience, the serving of Donnington ales and pub-grub sourced from local suppliers. The garden overlooks the Windrush. 01451 844385 (93/L2) foxingbarrington.com

Tunnel House Inn, Coates. A rural pub at the bottom of a pot-holed country lane. Worth the hazards for fine ales and the friendly ambience. Lies beside the Thames & Severn Canal. Children's play area. Dog friendly. Small camping area. 01285 770280 (8991/L9) tunnelhouse.com

Victoria Inn, Eastleach. A traditional country pub since 1856 that has been sensitively restored without losing its character. Great pub-grub and Arkells ales combine to make your visit a pleasure in keeping with the beauty of the pastoral landscape. Large beer garden suitable for muddy walkers, dogs and unkempt children. 01367 850277. (93/L6)

Woolpack Inn, Slad. A traditional Cotswold pub with wholesome food, simply cooked and home to a cup of Rosie's cider and the spirit of the late Laurie Lee. Newspapers, a pastoral view, Beer Fest, cricketers. No food on Mondays. 01452 813429 (90/F5) thewoolpackslad.com

Russell's of Broadway ss

Le Champignon Sauvage, 24-26 Suffolk Road, Cheltenham. A two Michelin starred restaurant with a reputation for their original approach to serving fine cuisine. Hence, no smartphones in the Dining Room. Whoopee! Two-Three set courses for lunch and dinner. The husband and wife team of David and Helen Everett-Matthias have maintained a reputation the envy of their peers for some 30-years. It has been accoladed as one of the top 10 foodie destinations in Britain. Open Tu-Sa (orders taken) 12.10-1.15, 7.30-8.30.01242 573449 (101/K7) lechampignonsauvage. co.uk

Curry Corner, 133 Fairview Road, Cheltenham. If you enjoy Indian cuisine stop here for some nourishment and hospitality. The Krori family have been delighting their customers for nigh on 40 years. Takeaways, too. Open Tu-Su 5.30-10.30. 01242 528449 (101/L7) thecurrycorner.com

Feathered Nest, Nether Westcote, Burford. This is very much a Restaurant within a pub that has been extended, transformed into a successful business. Well off the beaten track (nearby is the A424 Burford to Stow road), the owners have taken an entrepreneurial risk with their investment and have by all accounts fulfilled their desires. Very much a foodie's destination and one to add to your list of Top Restaurants/Inns. Oxfordshire ales to sup and drink beside a warm fire. In its early days the decor appeared a little contrived and the proprietors weren't prepared to give this writer a minute of their time. This irked me for manners are everything in my book. However, my daughter and I did enjoy their hot chocolate - which we paid for (as always)! 01993 833030 (99/M8) thefeatherednestinn.co.uk

5 North Street, Winchcombe. Has gained a healthy respect from fellow restaurateurs in the Cotswolds. You have a small and well-run restaurant with low-beamed ceiling in a quaint C17 building providing a relaxed and friendly atmosphere. 01242 604566 (98/B4) 5northstreetrestaurant.co.uk

Koj, 3 Regent St., Cheltenham. Some have described this empire of foodie delights as an Asian café. The proprietor has an impeccable record of Japanese heritage and experience of working in some top-notch kitchens; the Ledbury, Le Gavroche and Hestor Blumenthal. Andrew Kojima was also a finalist on Masterchef. Cocktail bar upstairs. 01242 580455 (101/K7) kojcheltenham.co.uk

Royal Oak, Whatcote. This is the ultimate Dining Pub, or really a smart restaurant within a pub build. Richard Craven will pepper your taste buds to Kingdom Come and back and you will ask for more, encore, until your hedonism explodes like the Savant in *La Grande Bouffe*. Game in season, fish from Cornwall, cheeses from Neals Yard. Closed Monday and Tuesdays. 01295 688100 (106/D5) theroyaloakwhatcote.co.uk

Russell's, 20 High St., Broadway. This has gained quite a reputation as a great place to eat in the North Cotswolds. So, feast on their food, then settle into one of their contemporary, comfy bedrooms with all the latest mod cons and indulge yourselves. Fish and chip shop, behind. 01386 853555 (104/F9) russellsofbroadway. co.uk

The Butchers Arms, Eldersfield. Are you on a quest to discover the perfect pub-grub nosh? Look no further. Local vegetables, beef from a locally reared herd of Hereford cattle and Wye Valley ales. A set menu Tu-Th & F lunchtime. The Block family will have you purring with delight. Treat yourself. 01452 840381 (100/C3) thebutchersarms.net

The Old Butchers, 7 Park Street, Stow-On-The-Wold. This is a family-run business (Peter and Louise Robinson) that has kept Cotswold folk who adore seafood and a carnivorous feast accompanied by fine wines, in the pink, and happy for many years. Open all week for lunch and dinner. 01451 831700 (99/K5) theoldbutchers.squarespace.com

Koj, Cheltenham ss

EAT... DRINK... SLEEP...

Angel, 14 Witney Street, Burford. My local spies inform me this Inn serves the finest food in town. Its a relaxed, stylish brasserie in a C16 coaching inn with log fires and provides mouth-watering fare: Mediterranean dishes and enormous breakfasts are prepared for the adventurous Cotswold explorer. 01993 822714 (94/B3) theangelatburford.co.uk

Five Alls, Filkins. A comfortable and charming C18 coaching inn offers log fires, great nosh and luxurious bedrooms, and maybe, the odd celeb in mufty enjoying a Cotswold repast. 01367 860875 (92/A7) thefiveallsfilkins.co.uk

Old Passage (Inn), Arlingham. This restaurant with rooms has a magical and spellbinding quality. The restaurant is a light and airy space given to fine views across the Severn, only bettered by the view from the bedrooms above. This continues to be a sea-foodies delight: prawns, devilled whitebait, freshly shucked oyster, Pembrokeshire lobster, roast halibut, et al. Meat, too. Special 'Severn Bore' breakfasts. Closed Ms. 01452 740547 (108/B4) theoldpassage.com

Plough, The Green, Kingham. A long-term favourite of foodie aficionados in West Oxfordshire now under new ownership. You have the laid-back pub area serving local and draught ales and exceptional bar food. The dining room serves English Classic fare, and you have the 7-luxurious bedrooms. It's all a winning combination just awaiting your reservation. 01608 658327 (96/B6) thekinghamplough.co.uk

Red Lion, Long Compton. This is my local spies favourite, Rick, who was thrown out of The Swan at Swinbrook for complaining of inedible and under cooked lamb (echoing his neighbours experience on accompanying table). Rick finds this inn hard to fault for food, service, friendliness and atmosphere. I liked it, too, for its simple unpretentiousness. 4-Rooms to sleep in. 01608 684221 (96/C2) redlion-longcompton.co.uk

St Michaels Restaurant, Victoria Street, Painswick. This is where I stop for coffee and brunch when in Painswick. Matt has 30-years experience of providing mouth-watering food. He works to a brief of

Old Passage Inn ss

Wild Rabbit, Kingham ss

simplicity, quality ingredients and local produce. Overlooking the Churchyard the location is a delight and in summer you can sit outside watching the passersby. Open W-Su from 10 am. 01452 812712 (90/F4)
stmichaelsbistro.co.uk

Village Pub, Barnsley. A warren of little rooms serving ambitious pub food and local beers. Child/dog friendly. Part of the Barnsley House empire opposite so expect a professional touch. 01285 740421 (92/E6)
thevillagepub.co.uk

Wheatsheaf Inn, Northleach. A friendly C17 coaching inn that invites long hours beside the log fires and lazy mornings lounging in their luxurious, comfy beds. Lunch and suppers to be recommended. Book club. Music nights. Northleach has a very fine "Wool" church and is just off the Fosse Way so central for Cotswold tours and bike rides. 01451 860244 (93/G1) theluckyonion.com

Wild Rabbit, Church Street, Kingham. A Daylesford (Lady Bamford) creation (or warren, ha-ha) designed for the upwardly mobile Londoner, and or, media-type. It is all glass and showey food in prep whilst the clientele are busily monitoring their laptops and iPads. The saving grace, the log fire, comfy seating and classy bedrooms. 01608 658389 (96/B6)
thewildrabbit.co.uk

Plough, Kingham ss

21

Ettington Park Hotel ss

Bath Priory Hotel, Weston Road. The Priory epitomises luxury and efficiency. Comfortable rooms with delightful garden views from the windows + more. A Country House Hotel noted for its fine dining, all within a short walk to Bath's many attractions. A retreat, indeed, from the hurley-burley of England's second most visited city.   01225 331922 (86/D8) thebathpriory.co.uk

Bay Tree Hotel, Sheep Street, Burford. This is Burford's most luxurious hostelry, for that is what Inns/hotels were on this old coaching route, hostelries. It is traditional and charming with oak-panelled rooms, stone fireplaces and tapestries. Dinner can be formal and there is a secluded walled garden for pre-prandials and intimate conversation. 01993 822791 (94/B3) cotswold-inns-hotels.co.uk

Buckland Manor Hotel, Nr Broadway. The benchmark for the Country House Hotel: quiet, understated luxury set within a 10-acre garden of sweeping lawns amidst stunning countryside. A lovely, modest-minded contrast to the ephemeral boutique hotel; oak-panelled walls, oil paintings, porcelain, antiques and traditional fireplaces with roaring log fires and discreet staff on hand. There's a formal dress code for dinner - the exquisite cuisine deserves your respect. Displays of flowers in abundance. Open all year. (104/E10)

Cotswold House Hotel & Spa, The Square, Chipping Campden. The building is very fine, of gold Cotswold stone set overlooking the Town Square. Out back is a lovely garden where you can find peace. The stairwell is a feature to admire. Two restaurants; Fig Restaurant (formal) and Bistro On The Square, innovative and deliciously sublime. Two bars. Spa with 6-treatment rooms, hydrotherapy pool and aromatic steam room. 01386 840330 (105/H8) cotswoldhouse.com

Ettington Park Hotel, Nr Stratford-Upon-Avon. A flamboyant Victorian Gothic hotel noted for its rococo plasterwork and much admired for its architectural flavours. The recent renovations have extended its market to include various leisure and spa facilities. But, in all it's very much aimed at the corporate and wedding markets. A short distance by car to Stratford and Shakespeariana. 01789 450123 (106/C3) handpickedhotels.co.uk/ettingtonpark

Feathers Hotel, 16-20 Market Street, Woodstock.

This romantic C17 hotel has a labyrinth of rooms on all levels; the bedrooms are plush, intimate and hidden up narrow stairwells. The restaurant has been producing superb food for years. Add the log fires and antique furniture and it makes for a winning combination. Within easy walking distance of Blenheim Palace, a short drive to Oxford and the Cotswold hills. 01993 812291 (97/L10)
feathers.co.uk

Foxhill Manor, Farncombe Estate, Broadway.

The old (traditional architecture) meets the new (bespoke baths, and beds) in a titanic clash that will seduce all those seeking a hedonistic break. Your very own private Cotswold retreat. Only 8-luxurious rooms. Butler service. And, down a swirling drive you come to The Fish, an exclusive, up-market style of centre-parc. 01386 858000 thefishhotel.co.uk. All part of the Farncombe Estate, previously known as Group 4 who used to run HM Prisons. Demand a cell with a view! 01386 852711 (105/G9)
foxhillmanor.com

Lords of the Manor, Upper Slaughter.

Classy, well established country house hotel with C17 origins set in 8-acres of parkland. Child friendly. No dogs. The former home of the Reverend F E B Witts, Rector of this parish who wrote his famous chronicle of the C18, *'The Diary of a Cotswold Parson.'* Afternoon Teas. 01451 820243 (99/H7)
lordsofthemanor.com

Lower Slaughter Manor.

If you seek a hotel with style, and old-fashioned virtues, this perfectly proportioned C17 Cotswold manor house may well be to your liking. There are large, spacious rooms furnished with antiques and classic art. No children U-12. No dogs. and classic art. No children U-12. No dogs. 01451 820456 (99/J7)
lowerslaughter.co.uk

The Painswick, Kemps Lane.

This lovely Palladian-style Cotswold rectory has been transformed back into a comfortable country house hotel with contemporary furnishings, feastings of lovely food and various hedonistic treatments. The perfect location for a weekend without your car and multiple circular walks. 01452 813688 (90/F4)
thepainswick.co.uk

Lower Slaughter Manor

SPA HOTELS

Barnsley House & Spa, Nr Cirencester. The former home of the garden expert, the late Rosemary Verey. A chic hotel and spa offering discreet and friendly service, great food and state-of-the-art technology. A visit to this extraordinary garden may cost you lunch but it will be a worthwhile and memorable experience. Make sure you visit the vegetable garden. Cinema club. 01285 740000 (92/E6) barnsleyhouse.com

Calcot Manor & Spa, Nr Tetbury. This is a leisure complex combining an English country house hotel furnished in contemporary, up-to-the-minute designs, that flow with ease into the C14 Cistercian barns and all ideally suited for a family, business or leisurely stay. Adjacent, you have Calcot Spa for health, beauty and relaxation - for pampering the Self. And if, after all this hedonism, you need some simple refreshment, a glass of ale or some nourishment then pop next door, to the Gumstool Inn. Location is ideal for exploring the southern Cotswolds, and Bath. 01666 890391 (88/E3) calcotmanor.co.uk

Combe Grove Hotel & Spa, Nr Bath. An C18 manor house set in 76-acres of woodland that is becoming a Retreat from this crazy world, a Fitness Club with Spa treatments to enliven your sensory glands where you can indulge in some much-needed rest, wholesome foods, healthy drinks and their holistic treatments, and all overlooking a stupendous English landscape. 01225 834644 (86/E10) combegrove.com

Cowley Manor & Spa, Nr Cheltenham. A chic, and stylish (unstuffy) country hotel, set in 55-acres with four lakes and a Victorian cascade. Techno-gadgets galore. Child-friendly (including Play Stations). A Spa with all the pampering (and more) that you may well need in this crazy world. A Church if you seek Wedlock and best of all, friendly staff. Popular pub within walking distance - The Green Dragon. 01242 870900 (91/L2) cowleymanor.com

Dormy House Hotel & Spa, Farncombe Estate, Broadway. C17 farmhouse converted into a comfortable hotel with a multitude of leisure facilities. Adjacent, an 18-hole golf course. Popular dining room and barn owl bar.01386 852711 (105/G9) dormyhouse.co.uk

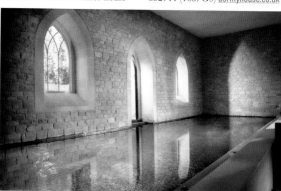

Royal Crescent Hotel & Spa, Bath ss

Calcot Manor ss

Ellenborough Park Hotel, Southam. If you seek space, style, spa treatments and affable staff with local knowledge, all within jumping distance of Cheltenham's Racecourse it is all here within a 90-acre estate. At its heart a Cotswold manor house dating back to the 1500s surrounded by sweeping lawns and new buildings quarried from a local quarry to provide authenticity and the wow factor. The bedrooms are luxurious and contemporary, the food is of a very high quality. Dogs welcome. 01242 545454 (101/L6) ellenboroughpark.com

Lygon Arms & Spa, High Street, Broadway. This is a former coaching inn of renown that has recently been re-branded into a luxurious Spa, and Country House Hotel. The centrepiece is the Great Hall with imposing barrel-vaulted ceiling, C17 Minstrel's Gallery, suits of armour and oak panels, and off the hall are cosy lounges with log fires and deep armchairs. Many additional, contemporary rooms, but when you book ask for a traditional bedroom. 01386 852255 (104/F9) lygonarmshotel.co.uk

The Royal Crescent Hotel & Spa, 16 Royal Crescent, Bath. The Royal Crescent occupies two listed buildings which were built by John Wood the Younger and have remained fairly unchanged since the C18. This makes a perfect setting for what is an extravagantly luxurious hotel full of period details. Step into the Royal and you enter a more sumptuous world - one of overstated luxury. Rooms are filled with period details and paintings from C18 masters. Behind the hotel lies a surprise - the beautiful and secluded gardens, perfect for afternoon tea, and overlooked by the "Dower House" restaurant and bar. The former coach houses are now the Bath House Spa. 01225 823333 (86/D8) royalcrescent.co.uk

Thyme Estate, Southrop. A "Spa" destination that has created a village of hedonism for the wealthy and style-minded. There is The Swan, a dining pub that could well-be the entrance for Alice into her Looking Glass where she will discover a Cookery School, luxury B&B, Private Dining, cottages to hire for individuals and house parties. The food is provided by the kitchen garden and farm belonging to the Thyme and Southrop Manor Estate. 01367 850205 (93/L7) thyme.co.uk

Wyck Hill House Hotel & Spa, Nr Stow-On-The-Wold. An impressive build of Cotswold stone overlooking the beautiful, dreamlike Windrush Valley and rolling Cotswold hills. There are 60-bedrooms and some have French-style furnishings in the Featured Bedrooms. All about you are wood-pannelled rooms, open fires and antique furnishings that delivers an Old-School style co-existing with a modern Spa featuring 6-treatment rooms, a sauna and a relaxation area set within 50-acres of grounds for you to wander aimlessly. 01451 831936 (99/K7) wyckhillhousehotel.co.uk

Swan Hotel, Bibury

Bradley Hotel, 19 Bayshill Road, Cheltenham. This is an intimate boutique-style hotel within the heart of this elegant Cotswold town. The decor is sumptuous and a little over-the-top and the location aa stone's throw to the finest shopping street in England. Dog friendly. Special weekend breaks. B&B only. 01242 519077 thebradleyhotel.co.uk

Close Hotel, Long Street, Tetbury. This is a traditional Cotswold hotel that has been transformed into the present day with contemporary furnishings, decor and a smart bar. Lunch can be exceptional value and a comfortable chair awaits you in their lovely garden whilst you look forward to your afternoon tea. 01666 502272 (91/G3) cotswold-inns-hotels.co.uk

Dial House, High Street, Bourton-On-The-Water. A small, intimate hotel with individually designed bedrooms. Informal lunches, candlelit dinners, roaring log fires and romantic rooms are all for your pleasures.

Not forgetting that it's nicely tucked away (from the hordes of Bourton visitors) within a large garden. 01451 822244 (99/J8) dialhousehotel.com

Kings Hotel, The Square, Chipping Campden. Handsome Cotswold hotel and brasserie with spacious interior. Drop in for their delicious breakfast, as I did pre-walk. Chic bedrooms. French-ambience to decor. 01386 840256 (105/H8) kingscampden.co.uk

Noel Arms Hotel, Lower High Street, Chipping Campden. A C16 coaching inn that has been transformed into a luxurious contemporary hotel: it's all log fires, four-posters and fine ales. Event Nights; curry, Mexican, beer…to keep you wanting more. 01386 840317 (105/H8) noelarmshotel.com

No. 131 The Promenade, Cheltenham. You really can't find a better location than this venue in this Regency town. Smack opposite Imperial Gardens and a short walk onto the finest shopping street in England. The rooms are all independently decorated and designed with locally sourced materials. Lavish and a wee bit over the top but good fun. And, not forgetting the stupendously popular restaurant Crazy Eights in the basement. For something a little more intimate, try their little sister at **No. 38 Evesham Road.** 01242 822939 (101/K7) theluckyonion.com

Old Bell Hotel, Abbey Row, Malmesbury. England's oldest purpose built hotel dating back to 1220. A fine place to stay if you seek comfort coupled with historic charm. Dine in the formal Edwardian Restaurant, or the less formal Hanks Room. Next door, Malmesbury Abbey the burial place in 941 AD of Athelstan, the first King of all England. 01666 822344 (89/J6) oldbellhotel.co.uk

Porch House, Digbeth Street, Stow-On-The-Wold. Claims to be the oldest Inn in England, dating from 947 AD. It has a had a complete make-over and a new name. It is thus, now a luxurious hostelry; cosy and comfy, backed up by fine dining. 13-bedrooms. Adjacent, The Pub and Conservatory for informality. 01451 870048 (99/K5) porch-house.co.uk

Rectory, Crudwell. This is a really lovely C16 house that has been transformed into a small, comfortable country house hotel with 12-bedrooms. Three acres with Victorian walled garden, croquet lawn and heated, outdoor swimming pool. Beauty and Health therapies on hand. Noted, however, for its cuisine. 01666 577194 (89/L4) therectoryhotel.com

Swan Hotel, Bibury. Few hotels have such a fabulous location as this which overlooks the River Coln brimming with trout . Photographed by every Bibury visitor, it is an iconic site. Café Swan (brasserie). Fishing rights. 18-luxurious bedrooms. 01285 740695 (93/G5) cotswold-inns-hotels.co.uk

Porch House, Stow-on-the-Wold ss

BED & BREAKFAST

Abbots Grange, Church Street, Broadway. If you seek one of the most romantic hideaways in the Cotswolds this may well fulfil all your desires. Step back in time to Medieval England and a Manor House built c.1320 but with the comforts of the C21. 4-poster beds, log fires, Great Hall, croquet lawn, tennis court, parkland, rose gardens and helicopter pad. A mere 2-3 minutes walk to the village of Broadway. Breakfast, no Dinner. 02081 338698 (104/F9) abbotsgrange.com

Cardynham House, Tibbiwell Street, Painswick. A luxurious B&B set within an enchanting C15-16 former wool merchant's home. Each room is individually decorated from 'Old Tuscany' to 'Cottage Rose' but if you seek a real treat try the 'Pool Room'. Bistro. 01452 814006 (90/F4) cardynham.co.uk

Clapton Manor, Clapton-on-the-Hill. Stunning Grade II listed Tudor house with a beautiful garden created by your host - a garden designer, and historian who have been doing B&B for 22-years. Fab breakfasts of homemade bread, eggs, Gloucester Old Spot sausages and fruit compotes are either made on the premises or come from next door... 01451 810202 (99/J9) claptonmanor.co.uk

Cowley House, Church Street, Broadway. A C17 Cotswold stone house offering luxurious accommodation and olde world charm. Within walking distance of the Village Green. 01386 858148 (104/F9) cowleyhouse-broadway.co.uk

Eckington Manor, Hammock Road, Eckington. Believed to be one of the oldest houses in Worcestershire. A period house full of character that has been renovated with emphasis on quality and style. There are 17-bedrooms spread over four converted farm buildings: Lower End House, The Cyder Mill, The Grain Barn and Milking Parlour. Each one available to book individually or for a group or family. Perfectly located for walking on the nearby Bredon or Malvern Hills. Restaurant and state of the art Cookery School. 01386 751600 (103/J7) eckingtonmanor.co.uk

Frampton Court, Frampton-On-Severn. A Grade I Vanbrugh

House, garden and family home. Fine panelling, original furniture and porcelain, 1732. Superb Gothic C18 garden building, The Orangery for self-catering accommodation (sleeps 8). Fine landscaping with park, lake and ornamental canal. Home of the 'The Frampton Flora' a famous wild flower painting. C16 Wool Barn for hire. Country fair in September. Available for B&B & House Parties. Across the Village Green you have Frampton Manor. A Grade I timber-framed medieval Manor House with walled garden and barn. C12 Birthplace of 'Fair Rosamund' Clifford, mistress to Henry II. House and garden open by written appointment, for groups of 10, or more. 01452 740698 (108/E5) framptoncourtestate.co.uk

Lypiatt House Hotel, Lypiatt Road, Cheltenham. A stylish boutique hotel adorned with contemporary furnishings set off with sumptuous fabrics, all within a short walk of Cheltenham's Montpelier district. There are 12-bedrooms to choose from with the additional mod-cons and a full breakfast is an option. 01242 224994 (101/K8) lypiatt.co.uk

Mill Hay House, Snowshill Road, Broadway. An imposing and elegant Queen Anne house surrounded by a stunning garden provides luxurious accommodation on the outskirts of Broadway. All three bedrooms have super king-size beds. Gourmet breakfasts to set you up for a Cotswold tour, starting at Broadway Tower. No children U-12. No dogs. 01386 852498 (104/F10) millhay.co.uk

No.12 Park Street, Cirencester. If style and gracious comfort is to your liking then this Grade II Georgian townhouse offering luxurious B&B may be just what you are looking for. 01285 640232 (92/B8) no12cirencester.co.uk

Oak House No1 Hotel, The Chipping, Tetbury. An extravaganza of sumptuous decadence and wild decor were you can realise your fantasies (of Arabian Nights?) and have that crazy weekend you have always dreamed of. What you get is that personal touch so missing from many hospitality units. Full techie stuff on offer; Wifi, Sky TV, Bluetooth etc…but will you really need it when on offer is…? 01666 505741 (89/G3) oakhouseno1.com

Oak House, Tetbury ss

Cotswold Farm Park, Nr Bourton-On-The-Water.

A recent development with 40 pitches on a two-acre level, grassy site. All the expected mod cons are provided plus a shop stocking freshly baked bread and local farm produce. Adam's Kitchen also offers homemade cakes, light lunches and snacks. And, you have moo cows to wake you up and the odd Cock crowing. 01451 850307 (98/F5) cotswoldfarmpark.co.uk

Cotswold View Caravan & Camping Park, Charlbury.

A popular well run site in the Oxfordshire Cotswolds. All within 54 acres of rolling, wooded farmland. Ideal for walking, cycling and touring the many attractions close by. Tennis court. Shop. 01608 810314 (97/G8) cotswoldview.co.uk

Denfurlong Farm, Chedworth.

A basic site on a green field takes you back to nature. No showers. Dogs allowed. Good value. Farm shop and café with breakfast from 9. Dogs OK. Friday is fishn'chip night. Open March to October. 01285 720265 (92/D4)

Far Peak Camping, Northleach.

A simple campsite set in the middle of the Cotswolds, beside the Roman Fosse Way and all within walking distance of Northleach. Café. Cycle Hire and Climbing Wall. 01285 720858 (90/F2) farpeakcamping.co.uk

Fireside Glamping, Westley Farm, Cowcombe Hill, Chalford.

80-acre hill farm of ancient woodlands, flower-rich hay meadows, and steep banks of limestone grassland with traditional stone (self-catering) cottages spread over the hillside. For the more adventurous try one of the two Turkoman style yurt tents situated

Fireside Glamping, Chalford ss

in the diddly-dumps. 07519 883232 91/H8) westleyfarm.co.uk

Folly Farm Campsite, Nr Bourton-On-The- Water. Set high on the Central Wolds in a draftie and healthy spot. Ideal for tents and the simple life. Don't expect 5 star accommodation. 01451 820285 (99/G8) cotswoldcamping.net

Hayles Fruit Farm, Winchcombe. Set in a quiet rural location beside Hailes Abbey and the Cotswold Way so ideal for backpackers. Café/farm shop, on site. 01242 602123 (98/D4) haylesfruitfarm.co.uk

Organic Farm Shop, Burford Road, Cirencester. A Green Field site with lovely views set within this organic farm. Their dictum 'Eating organic is eating from the Earth, Back to nature

void of pesticides. All growing freely without insecticides.' Café. 01285 640441 (92/C7) theorganicfarmshop.co.uk

Thistledown Environment Centre, Nympsfield. An organic camp site that promotes the awareness of agricultural and environmental practices by tackling ecological issues head on in a fun way. Follow the adventure, sculpture and wildlife trails. Farm shop and Fieldfare Café. Dogs allowed. 01453 860420 (90/C8) thistledown.org.uk

Tunnel House Inn, Coates. A rural pub with a great ambience, fine ales and yummy food has a number of small pitches and lies in an idyllic location beside the Thames and Severn Canal. Children's play area. Dogs welcome. 01285 770280 (91/L9) tunnelhouse.com

Belas Knap Long Barrow

Bagendon Earthworks.
Remains of the Dobunni tribes'
headquarters which was the capital
of the Cotswolds in the C1 AD.
The settlement was abandoned ten
years after the Roman Conquest.
Iron Age silver coins excavated
here. (92/B6)

Barrow Wake, Birdlip. Deep
scarp edge. Favourite viewpoint.
Roman pottery found at the
bottom of scarp. Car park. (91/J1)

Belas Knap Long Barrow. In
Old English translates 'beacon
mound'. A burial chamber, 4,000
years old. Opened in 1863 to
reveal 38 skeletons. In superb
condition and good viewpoint.
Steep footpath from road. Beside
the Cotswold Way. (98/B6)

Bredon Hill Fort. Iron Age
fort with two ramparts and
scene of great battle at time of
Christ possibly against the Belgic
invaders. The hacked remains
of 50 men were found near the
entrance. Superb views over to
Wales, Vale of Evesham, the rivers
Severn and Avon, and to the
Cotswolds. (103/K8)

Grim's Ditch, Blenheim.
Disconnected series of ditches
and banks built by Iron Age
tribes (Belgic) to defend their
grazing enclosures. Best sections
in Blenheim and Ditchley Parks.
Grim is one of the names of
Woden – the masked one, the
god of victory, death and magic

power, the high god of the Anglo-
Saxons before their conversion to
Christianity in the C7. (97/K8))

Hetty Pegler's Tump. Neolithic
Long Barrow 120ft x 22ft, 4
chambers, 38 skeletons found in
C19. Torch and Wellington boots
needed. (90/B9)

Uley Bury Iron Age Hill Fort.
This is the Cotswolds most famous
Iron Age site. The deep ramparts
provide superb views across the
Severn Vale, Welsh Hills, Dursley
and Owlpen Woods. It's an
enclosed area of about 32-acres
and is used for arable crops.
Of more interest, it has an easy
circular walk possible for large
wheeled pushchairs. (90/B9)

Meon Hill, Mickleton. An Iron-
age hill fort to which the locals
keep well away from for fear of the
spookery of witchcraft. (105/J5)

**Nan Tow's Tump, Nr
Leighterton.** A Long Barrow.
9ft high and 100ft in Diameter
crowned with trees. Believed to
contain skeleton of Nan Tow, a
local Witch buried upright. (88/C5)

**Rollright Stones, Nr Chipping
Norton.** The King's Men is a
Bronze Age stone circle 100 feet
in diameter, 2,000-1,800 BC and
is easily accessible from the road.
Just 400 yards east of this circle are
The Whispering Knights, remains
of a Bronze Age burial chamber.
And, isolated in a field, the King's
Stone. (96/D3)

Akeman Street. Roman road built to provide communications between military units and their forts. Best seen near Coln St Aldwyn and Quenington. (92/F7)

Corinium Dobunorum. The second Largest Roman town after London Londinium. Amphitheatre on Querns Hill and villas hereabouts. See the Corinium Museum for details. (92/B8)

Ermin Way. Roman road linking Cirencester with Gloucester and Kingsholm; two encampments on the edge of Roman civilisation. Built and manned by troops. This undulating road still leaves a marked pattern across the landscape. (91/L4)

Fosse Way. The famous Roman road linking Exeter with Lincoln that runs diagonally across the Cotswold escarpment. One can still see evidence of Staging Posts and Bakehouses beside the road. (92/D5)

North Leigh Roman Villa (EH), Nr Woodstock. This ruin was excavated in 1813 and 60 rooms were revealed surrounding the courtyard with a beautiful mosaic pavement. A charming spot beside the River Evenlode. Open daily in summer. (95/J1)

Salmonsbury Camp, Bourton-On-The-Water. The Romans' second legion of 5,000 soldiers was encamped here and built Lansdown Bridge to ford the Windrush on the Fosse Way. (99/K8)

Spoonley Roman Villa, Nr Winchcombe. Excavated in 1882. What few remains there are, are not clearly visible. The site lies on private property with a footpath passing nearby. (98/C5)

Witcombe Roman Villa (EH), Nr Gloucester. Discovered by workmen whilst removing an ash tree. Later excavated in 1818 and 1935. Dates from C1 AD and occupied until the C4. Tessellated Pavements, mosaics and Bath Wing. Closed to view. (91/H2)

Wortley Roman Villa, Nr Wotton. Believed to be in existence from the C1 to C4. It was accidentally discovered in 1981 when an archaeological dig by the University of Keele unveiled Roman and Saxon coins, painted wall plaster, pottery and a damaged hypocaust. Much is on display in Stroud Museum. (88/A4)

Woodchester Roman Villa, Church Lane. This huge villa was excavated by Lysons in 1993 and revealed 64 rooms including the Orpheus Pavement. Today, there is little to see. The pavement lies buried and plans to uncover it lie dormant. (90/E7)

Mosaic of Spring, Chedworth Roman Villa

Bath Abbey. The Church of St Peter and St Paul has seen three churches occupy this site: an Anglo-Saxon church in 757 and a Norman Cathedral in 1090 but later in 1137 much of this was destroyed by fire. Today's building was founded in 1499 to replace the ruin damaged in the fire. But, it had again to be rebuilt in 1611 following Henry VIII's *Dissolution of the Monasteries*. In simple architectural terms it can be described as Perpendicular Gothic and cruciform in plan. The fan vaulting of the Nave is very fine and was designed by Robert and William Vertue designers of Henry VII's chapel in Westminster Abbey. It was never finished until Gilbert Scott completed the original designs in the 1860s. Note the Stairway to Heaven on the West Front: two ladders of carved angels are climbing towards Christ. Tower Tours. Open daily 9-6. 01225 422462 (86/D8) bathabbey.org

Bruern Abbey, Nr Bledington. The present building, a school, was built on the site of a Cistercian abbey established in 1147 and dissolved in 1536. A vaulted chamber is all that remains (within a Georgian cottage) in the grounds. (96/B8)

Cirencester Abbey. Only the Abbey grounds remain. A peaceful enclave behind the Parish Church of St John the Baptist. Open daily. (92/B8)

Gloucester Cathedral. The Cathedral Church of St Peter and the Holy and Undivided Trinity. Without exception the most magnificent building in Gloucestershire and one of the finest of all English cathedrals. The building's foundation stone was laid down by Abbot Serlo in 1089 on the site of a religious house founded by Osric, an Anglo-Saxon prince living here in about 678-9 AD. The Nave was completed in 1130. Its architecture is Romanesque with some early Perpendicular. The reconstruction of the Quire followed the burial in 1327 of Edward II. The East Window behind the altar had at its installation the largest display of medieval stained glass in the world and dates from 1350. The same year, fan vaulting was invented here at Gloucester and its intricate design covers the roof of the cloisters. Some would argue that Gloucester also saw the birth of Perpendicular architecture. In the South Transept survives the oldest of all Perpendicular windows. Allow a couple of hours to wander around this spiritual hot house. There are tours of the crypt and tower. You will also be shown the location used for part of *Hogwarts* in the Harry Potter films. Evensong is a most magical experience not to be missed as is the Christmas Carol service. Restaurant. Open daily 7.30am to 6pm. 01452 528095 (100/D9) gloucestercathedral.org.uk

Hailes Abbey(EH). Built in 1246 by Richard, Earl of Cornwall, brother of Henry III, having vowed he would found a religious house if he survived a storm at sea. Museum. The abbey became a popular place of pilgrimage in the Middle Ages until Henry VIII closed it down. It remains an attractive ruin with many surviving artefacts on display in the museum. Open daily Apr to Oct 31 10-5 01242 602398 (98/C3) englishheritage.org.uk

Kingswood Abbey Gatehouse, Nr Wotton-Under-Edge. The few remains of a C16 Cistercian abbey dissolved in 1538. (85/E4)

Malmesbury Abbey Church of St Peter & St Paul. Founded as a Benedictine Monastery in 676 AD by the saintly and scholarly

Tewkesbury Abbey

Brother Aldhelm. King Athelstan was buried here in 941 AD. By the C11 the monastery held the second largest library in Europe and was a place of learning and pilgrimage. The Abbey was built and completed by 1180. The tall spire rose to 431 feet (131m) and was to be seen for miles around. However, in 1500 it collapsed destroying the Nave and the Transept. A few years later in 1550 the West Tower also collapsed. What you see today is less than half of the original structure. Yet it still remains a formidable church and a sight to behold. It was also a place of great inspiration for in 1010 the monk Eilmer of Malmesbury became the first man to fly by jumping off the roof of the Tower and flying his hang glider 200 yards before crashing and breaking both his legs – Leonardo da Vinci was to design a similar machine 350 years later. Open daily 9-5 (-4 winter). (89/J6) malmesburyabbey.com

Pershore Abbey. Established in the late C10 by Benedictines. C14 tower and the superb vaulting of the Prestbytery remain. Beautiful Early English Choir but sadly much was destroyed by Henry VIII. Visitor Centre summer weekends. Look out for the intricate wooden sculpture in the grounds. Open daily 8-5.30. 01386 552071 (103/K5) pershoreabbey.fsnet.co.uk

Prinknash Abbey. Benedictine Monastery with C14 and C15 origins set amidst an idyllic rolling landscape. Abbey church opens 6am to 8.30pm. Monastery garden with possible Tudor origins. Café/shop open daily 10-5. Grounds open daily. 01452 812455 (89/G2) prinknashabbey.org.uk

Tewkesbury Abbey. Founded in 1087 by the nobleman Robert Fitzhamon. However, the present building was started in 1102 to house Benedictine monks. The Norman abbey was consecrated in 1121. The Nave and roof finished in the C14 in the Decorated style. Much is Early English and Perpendicular, although it is larger than many cathedrals and has according to Pevsner 'the finest Romanesque Tower in England'. The Abbey opens its doors to three major music festivals: Musica Deo Sacra, the Three Choirs Festival and the Cheltenham Music Festival. You can park opposite and take a tour. Info on 01684 850959. Shop and refectory. Open daily 8.30am to 5.30pm (W & F from 7.30am). (101/G2) tewkesburyabbey.org.uk

St James, Chipping Campden

Adderbury, St Mary. Early C13 cruciform. C14 West tower with massive carvings. Superb chancel and vestry. (105/M10)

Bloxham, St Mary. C14 spire. Carvings. C15 wall paintings. East window by William Morris and Edward Burne-Jones. (105/K10)

Burford, St John the Baptist. One of the great Cotswold churches built in the C15 with proceeds earned by the local wool merchants. Hence, the term 'Wool' church. It has a spacious interior more akin to a small cathedral. The porch and spire c.1450 are outstanding as are the sculptured table tombs in the churchyard. Inside don't miss the intricate medieval stained glass and the monuments (painted figures). Open daily 9-5 except during services. (92/B3)

Chipping Campden, St James. A fine old 'Wool' church, of Norman origin restored in the C15; with a tall and elegant tower and large Perpendicular nave. 'Brilliant' in late summer afternoons. C15 Cope, and a unique pair of C15 Altar Hangings. Brasses of Woolstaplers. C15 Falcon Lecturn. Open daily from 10. (103/H8)

Cirencester, St John the Baptist. A fine mix of the C14 and C15, the largest of the 'Wool' churches and the easiest to recognise with its three-storied, fan- vaulted porch. The porch formerly the Town Hall overshadows the Market Place. C15 'wine glass' pulpit, Ann Boleyn Cup and many fine brasses. Open M-Sa 9.30-5, Su in winter 2.15-5.30, in summer 12.30-6. (90/B8)

Fairford, St Mary the Virgin. The perfect, late C15 Perpendicular church that is world-famous for the outstanding 28 stained glass windows depicting

Gargoyle, St Peter, Winchcombe

scenes from Genesis to the Last Judgement. Of further interest are the carved misericords and recumbent brasses. Open 9.30-5.30 for visits and guided tours. 01285 712611 (91/H8)

Highnam, Holy Innocents. A Masterpiece of Victorian design and Thomas Parry's monument to his beloved, Isabella. Henry Woodyer (disciple of Pugin), Hardman and Parry completed this in 1851 with no expense spared; Wall paintings dominate the Nave, the floor with Minton tiles, the exterior with crockets and pinnacles. Open weekends. (98/B9)

Northleach, St Peter & St Paul. C15. The South Porch has been described as the most lovely in all England; Tall pinnacles and statue filled niches. From afar, the church appears to hover above the town. Brasses of wealthy wool barons. Guided tours: 01451 861172 (90/F2)

Painswick, St Mary. It is the soaring spire that will first captivate you, then as you enter, it will be the line of yew trees and then, as you wander around the churchyard, the tombs or monuments carved with their intricate figures. But do look up and admire the gold clock. The

St Peter & St Paul, Northleach

spire has been struck by lightning on many occasions in 1763 and 1883. The 100th yew tree always fades away. (88/F4)

Winchcombe, St Peter. One of the great 'Wool' churches. It is a C15 Perpendicular design but is strangely plain yet dignified. Not as elaborate as some of the other 'Wool' churches. For example, it has no chancel arch. The gargoyles are the one notable feature and a circumnavigation of the exterior is advised. The weathercock is the County's finest. (96/B4)

St John the Baptist, Burford

SMALLER CHURCHES

Berkeley, St Mary. One of Gloucestershire's most historic and interesting churches with a mass of features: Ring of ten bells, Norman doorway, C12 font, C13 chancel, C13-15 murals, C15 rood screen, C16 brass, Berkeley family tombs from the C15, and life-size effigies in alabaster, Jenner family vault and separate Gothic tower built in 1753. (85/B9) stmarys-berkeley.co.uk

Bibury, St Mary. If you seek a refuge from the hurly burly of Bibury's visitors then walk along the banks of the River Coln and you'll soon find the entrance to this pretty church. With evidence of Saxon remains, Norman font and superb sculptured table tombs. (91/G5)

Broadway, St Eadburgh's. A rare architectural gem of almost perfect proportions with a mix of C12-C18 additions. Superb brass work, topiary in churchyard, interesting tombstones and a welcome retreat from the hustle and bustle of Broadway. (102/F10)

Buckland, St Michaels. An exquisite church preserved with an almost undisturbed history from the C13 to the C17. Beautiful roof: painted and wood-panelled. C14 tower with gargoyles. C15 stained glass in East Window restored by William Morris. Not to be missed, the Wainscotting: medieval wooden benches along the far wall as you enter. The Hazel Bowl made in 1607 of Dutch maple with a silver rim. The Buckland Pall, C15 embroidered vestments from the V & A Museum, London. Sadly, the medieval frescoes were removed by the restorer FS Waller in 1885. (102/E10)

Deerhurst (Odda's Chapel). One of the few surviving Saxon chapels left in England. Earl Odda dedicated this rare chapel to the Holy Trinity on the 12th April 1056 in memory of his brother. Open daily. (98/F4)

Eastleach; Church of St Michael & St Martin. Founded by Richard Fitzpons, one of William the Conqueror's Knights. It has a C14 North transept, decorated windows and, a memorable exterior beside the river fronted by daffodils in spring. It closed for services in 1982, and the **Church of St Andrews** hidden beneath the trees is a tiny church with a more interesting interior than its neighbour. Note the splendid C14 saddleback-tower of a Transitional and Early English period style. (91/L6)

Oddington, St Nicholas. Medieval Doom painting. Jacobean pulpit. Beautiful, magical isolation half-a-mile from the village. (94/A6)

Swinbrook. Fettiplace monuments. Mitford family memorials. (92/C3)

Kelmscott. Wall painting. William Morris tomb by Philip Webb. (92/B9)

Wotton-Under-Edge, St Mary the Virgin. The first church on this site was probably destroyed by King John's mercenaries in the C11. The present structure was consecrated in 1283. Its Perpendicular tower, one of the county's finest has corner buttresses crowned with crocketed pinnacles. The marble tomb and the C15 brasses of Thomas, Lord Berkeley and his wife are outstanding. Note the C16 stained glass. Edward Barnsley in the Gimson tradition (*Arts & Crafts Movement*) designed the new altar and reredos on the north wall. The organ originally came from St. Martin in the Fields and had been a gift from George 1. George Handel played on it. Yet, the church lacks the beauty of Burford or Chipping Campden. (84/E3)

Bredon Barn

Ashleworth Tithe Barn. C15 with two projecting porch bays and a fine roof of timbers with Queenposts. Open daily dawn to dusk. 01451 814213 (98/C6)

Doughton Tithe Barn. Just across the road from Highgrove. This lies in the grounds of what I consider to be one of the most enchanting, unusual and beautiful of the Cotswolds many outstanding buildings. A VW Camper Van often peers through the doorway. (87/G5)

Enstone Tithe Barn, Rectory Farm. Dates from 1382 and is built with some magnificent timbers. (95/H6)

Frocester Court's Medieval Estate Barn. This is an enormous barn built between 1284 and 1306. It remains the second largest in England and is one of the best preserved with massive oak roof and is used every day by the farmer who owns it. For conducted tours: (of 5 or more) 01453 823250. (88/B7)

Higleadon Tithe Barn. Built in the C15 or C16 for the Abbey at Gloucester. It is a well-preserved late medieval barn with seven bays, close-studded timbers framing, Tudor arch and a stone-paved threshing floor. (98/B7)

Postlip Hall & Tithe Barn. A former Jacobean Manor House set in 15-acres. Postlip Hall has been for the past 40-years a co-housing idyll. Eight families live in separate dwellings, working the organic kitchen garden and grounds, and pursuing their own creative pleasures, be it writing, painting, sculpting or inventing. The original tithe barn is also in continual use except when it is hired out as a venue for weddings, parties and beer festivals. (96/A5)

Priors Court Tithe Barn, Brockworth. A C13 historic barn with vast oak beams and beautiful stone walls in use as a wedding venue. 01452 864486 (89/G1) priorscourtbarn.co.uk

Southam Tithe Barn. C14 or C15 with 8-bays and in need of renovation. I remember it well, the venue for my 21st Birthday Party. (99/L5)

Stanway Tithe Barn. This was designed in the C14 for Tewkesbury Abbey with the Golden Proportion in mind. It stands beside a pond in the grounds of the Manor House. Wedding venue. (96/D2)

Swalcliffe Barn. Early C15 tithe barn with fascinating displays of Oxfordshire's agricultural and trade vehicles. Exhibition of 2,500 years of the area. Open East Su to Oct Su & BH Ms 2-5. 01295 788278 (105/H9)

Blenheim Palace ss

Badminton House. The home of the Dukes of Beaufort and venue for the annual Badminton Horse Trials. The estate was bought by the Worcesters in 1682. It was the 3rd Duke who was responsible for the house as we see it today. First, he invited James Gibbs to set about remodelling the East and West wings, then William Kent finished the North Front in the Palladian style. Fox hunting has been a great passion of the Beauforts. Their early forebears hunted all the way to London and back. Publishing was another passion. From 1885 to 1902 they devised The Badminton Library of Sports & Pastimes - an aristocratic leather bound series of books that was like a combination of Punch and your High Street cricket or football magazine, albeit a little more high brow. And, of course, the game of Badminton was reintroduced here in 1873 following its Indian origins. The house is closed to the public. The closest you'll get is to visit during the Three Day Horse Trials. (88/C9)

Berkeley Castle. Home of the Berkeley family for the last 850 years. It remains a splendidly preserved Norman fortress with an enclosing curtain wall. Scene of Edward II's murder in 1327. Lovely terraced gardens. Superb Butterfly House. Open East to Oct Su-Th 11-5.30. 01453 810332 (87/B9) berkeley-castle.com

Blenheim Palace. The home of the Dukes of Marlborough was built as Queen Anne's gift to John Churchill 1st Duke of Marlborough for his defeat of Louis XIV in 1704, *'a monument to commemorate a military victory and to glorify the Queen'*. It is considered to be Vanburgh's C18 baroque masterpiece although much of thedetail was by Nicholas Hawksmoor. There are fine paintings, a Churchill Exhibition, tapestries, a 10,000 volume library and parkland designed by 'Capability' Brown. Plus, other attractions: the Butterfly House, Marlborough Maze, Adventure Play Area and Herb Garden. Restaurant.. Palace & Gardens open daily 10.30-5.30 (last add 4.45pm), Park open daily all year 9-6. 0800 84965500 (97/L10) blenheimpalace.com

Charlton Park. Palatial mansion built in 1607. Home to the Earls of Suffolk since the C16. There are 4,500 acres of arable and woodland with trout fishing and game shooting on hand. It is also the venue for WOMAD, the World of Music, Arts & Dance festival, with its own park and camp facility. 01666 822146 (89/K5) charltonpark.co.uk

Cheltenham, Pittville Pump Room. A masterpiece of C19 Greek Revivalism adorned with colonnaded facades, portico, pillared and balconied hall. Open daily, except during private functions. 01242 264231 (101/K7) pittvillepumproom.org.uk

Chipping Norton, Bliss Tweed Mill. Built by William Bliss in 1872 to house his textile factory. He was instrumental in encouraging the railways to reach Chipping Norton. The mill closed as a factory in 1980 and was converted into domestic apartments. It is still quite a sight from the road and was apparently one of Sir John Betjeman's favourite buildings. (96/D5)

Frampton Court. A Grade I Vanbrugh House, garden and family home. Fine panelling, original furniture and porcelain,1732. Superb Gothic C18 garden building, The Orangery for self- catering accommodation (sleeps 8). B&B. Fine landscaping with park, lake and ornamental canal. Home of the 'The Frampton Flora' a famous wild flower painting. C16 Wool Barn for hire. Country fair in September. 01452 740698 (87/E5) framptoncourtestate.co.uk

Sezincote House & Garden. House designed in the Indian style (and inspiration for the Brighton Pavilion) is beautifully set in an oriental water garden. House open May to Sept, Th F & BH Ms 2.30-5.30. Garden open Jan to Nov Th F & BH Ms 2-6. 01386 700444 (99/J3) sezincote.co.uk

Sudeley Castle. A Tudor house and the original home of the Seymour family. Katherine Parr, widow of Henry VIII lived here and lies buried in the chapel. There is a fine collection of needlework, furniture and tapestries plus paintings by Van Dyck, Rubens and Turner. All surrounded by award-winning gardens and open parkland. The Castle is open daily Apr to Oct 10.30-5. 01242 602308 (98/B5) sudeleycastle.co.uk

Woodchester Mansion. Be prepared for a good 1-mile walk from the car park down to this unfinished masterpiece of Victorian stone masonry set in a secret Cotswold valley. The restoration project is on-going and ambitious. Bat Exhibition. Open East-Oct most W/Es 11-5. 01453 861541 (90/C8)

Sezincote House & Garden ss

MANOR HOUSES

Broughton Castle. Moated medieval manor house, substantially enlarged in the C16. Magnificent plaster ceilings, fine panelling and fireplaces. Interesting Civil War connections. In the family of the Lords Saye and Sele for over 600 years. Multi-coloured borders. The location for much of the film, *Shakespeare in Love*. Open East & BHs, then W & Su May to mid- Sept, also Th in July & Aug 2-5. 01295 276070 (107/K9) broughtoncastle.com

Chavenage. A haunted Elizabethan manor house that has remained virtually unchanged for 400 years. A replica of a bygone age. It contains two complete tapestry rooms, furniture and relics of the Civil War. Guided tours by the family. George and Elizabeth Warleggan's family home in the *Poldark* TV saga. Specialises in weddings and corporate events. Open East Su & M, also May to Oct Th, Su & BHs 2-5. 01666 502329 (88/F2) chavenage.com

Compton Wynyates. A Tudor dream house built 1460 with multi-coloured bricks; pale rose, crimson, blood red, shades of orange and bluish brown. Twisted chimneys. Panelled rooms. Plaster ceilings. Perhaps, the most romantic of all England's country houses. Sadly no longer open. May be glimpsed through the trees from the nearby road. (106/F7)

Frampton Manor. Grade I timber framed medieval Manor House with walled garden and barn. C12 Birthplace of 'Fair Rosamund' Clifford, mistress to Henry II. House and garden open by written appointment for groups of 10 or more. Tours: 01452 740268. (108/E5)

Kelmscott Manor. The Elizabethan home of William Morris, the C19 poet, craftsman and socialist. Houses his furnishings which can be identified as examples from the *Arts & Crafts Movement*. Paintings by his fellow pre-Raphaelite, Dante Gabriel Rossetti. Open Apr to Oct W & Sa 11-5, Group visits on Th by arrangement. 01367 252486 (94/B9) kelmscottmanor.co.uk

Chavenage ss

Stanway House

Kingston Bagpuize House. A beautiful early C18 manor house in parkland setting. The garden contains shrubs, bulbs and herbaceous borders. Teas. Small gift shop. Open mid-May to mid-July M-Tu 1-6, Su 11-2. Gardens open more frequently. See website or phone for details. 01865 820259 (95/J10)
kingstonbagpuizehouse.org.uk

Owlpen Manor. An iconic group of picturesque Cotswold buildings: Manor House, Tithe Barn, Church, Mill and Court House. Water Garden and terrace. The Tudor manor dates from 1450 to 1616 but the whole estate has 900 of history to impart. Garden and Terrace open Apr-Sept M-F 12-5. Special Group Visits, & Weddings. Cottages for hire. 01453 860261 (990/C10) owlpen.com

Rodmarton Manor. This is a unique building built by Ernest Barnsley and his Cotswold group of craftsmen for the Biddulph family from 1909 to 1929. It displays Cotswold *"Arts and Crafts"* furniture, metalwork and wall hangings. The 8-acre garden is a series of outdoor rooms and is a marvel throughout the year. Refreshments. Opens for February snowdrops & East M, then May to Sept W, Sa & BHs 2-5. 01285 841253 (89/K1)
rodmarton-manor.co.uk

Stanton Harcourt Manor House & Gardens. A unique collection of medieval buildings. The house contains fine pictures, silver, furniture and porcelain. Moat and stew ponds. Pope's Tower. Open Apr-Sept as advertised. 01865 881928 (95/K6)

Stanway House & Water Garden. This exquisite Jacobean Manor House and Gatehouse is built from the local stone known as Guiting Yellow which lights up when the sun touches it. All is set within an enchanting and ancient parkland designed by a numerologist, the home of the Earl of Wemyss and March. The partially restored C18 Cascade and Canal was designed by the highly respected Charles Bridgman, and is now open June to Aug, Tu & Th 2-5. 01386 584469 (98/D2)
stanwayfountain.co.uk

Arlington Row

Arlington Row, Bibury. These Iconic cottages were originally monastic wool barns. However, in the C17 they were converted into weavers' homes. Now domestic dwellings, they overlook Rack Isle, a 4-acre water meadow where cloth was once hung out to dry. (93/G6)

Bredon Barn. A beautifully constructed large medieval threshing barn extending to 132 feet. Expertly restored after fire. Open daily 10-6, dusk if earlier. 01451 844257 (103/H9)

Buscot Park. C18 house with park and superb water garden designed by Harold Peto. Collection of art: Italian, Dutch, Flemish, Spanish and English Schools. Chinese porcelain. Tea room. Open Apr to Sept W Th & F (including Good F, East W/Es) 2-6, and alternate W/Es in each month 2-6. Grounds also M & Tu 2-6. 01367 240786 (94/A10)

Chedworth Roman Villa. Discovered in 1864 by a local gamekeeper and later excavated between 1864 and 1866 revealing remains of a Romano-British villa containing mosaics, baths and hypocausts. Family trails. Museum. Open daily mid-Feb to end Nov from 10. 01242 890256 (92/D2)

Dyrham Park. C17 William and Mary mansion house set in a deer park with elegant formal gardens. The house belonged to the family of Sir William Blathwayt's wife, Mary Wynter. Blathwayt was secretary of war to William III (1671-1720). Sir William started to remodel the dilapidated Tudor mansion on site in 1692-1699. Victorian domestic quarters, Splendid collection of Dutch paintings. Film location for *'Remains of the Day'* (1993). Open March to 2 Nov daily. Park open all year. 0117 9372501 (86/C3)

Farnborough Hall. A beautiful honey-coloured stone house sits in parkland crated in the 1740s. Noted for the exquisite C18 plasterwork. Parkland walks and lake views. Open Apr to Sept W & Sa 2-5.30. 01295 690002 (107/L3)

Hidcote Manor Garden. One of the finest gardens of the C20 designed by Major Lawrence Johnston in the *Arts & Crafts* style. It is made up of garden rooms with rare trees, shrubs, herbaceous borders and 'old' roses. The all-weather court has recently been restored. Barn café and plant sales opens at 10. Garden open daily Mid-Feb & Nov-Dec 11-4, Mar to Oct 10-dusk. 01386 438333 (105/J7)

Chastleton House

Lodge Park. A 'little' property with a big (boozy) history. A grandstand (folly) built by John 'Crump' Dutton in 1634 so he could watch deer coursing in comfort and share his passion for gambling, drinking and entertaining with his friends. Open Feb 1/2 term W/Es, Mar to May & Oct F-Su 11-4 & M in June-Sept. 01451 844130 (93/H3)

Middle Littleton Tithe Barn. This C13 barn is considered one of the finest in the country with ten bays and 130 feet long. Open daily Apr to Oct 2-5. 01905 371006 (104/E4)

Snowshill Manor & Garden. A Cotswold manor house containing Charles Paget Wade's extraordinary collection of craftsmanship and design amounting to some 22,000 items; from toys to musical instruments, Samurai armour to clocks and bicycles. Open daily mid-Mar to Oct 12-5. Grounds, restaurant and shop from 11. 01386 852410 (98/F2)

Upton House & Gardens. This house exhibits the lifestyle of a 1930s millionaire. It also has an outstanding display of English and Continental Old Masters paintings plus a wealth of herbaceous borders, terraces and tranquil water gardens. Open most days. See website for details. 01295 670266 (107/G5)

Snowshill Manor

ARBORETA & GARDENS

Abbey House Gardens, Malmesbury. The naturist home of the Naked Gardener, so be prepared for a surprise and some excitement amidst the tulips! View their website for Clothes Optional Days. There are bulbs galore especially the 70,000 tulips in Spring and a massive range of 2,200 different roses, herbaceous borders, specimen trees and shrubs. Open daily 21 Mar to 21 Oct 11-5.30. 01666 822212 (89/ J6) abbeyhousegardens.co.uk

Batsford Arboretum & Garden Centre. 56-acres of rare and beautiful trees are part of one of the largest private collection of trees in Britain. The Japanese Cherry blossom are stunning in April. Open daily from 9 (10 on Su & BHs). 01386 701441 (99/K2) batsarb.co.uk

Bourton House Garden. 3-acres of intense planting; topiary, knot garden, potager and a profusion of herbaceous borders and exotic plants. The wonderful tithe barn is host to a gallery of contemporary arts and crafts. Lunches and teas. Pre-booked groups only. Open Apr-Oct Tu-F 10-5. Lunches/teas from May. 01386 700754 (99/K2) bourtonhouse.com

Cerney House Gardens, North Cerney. Just look around and you know it has been created by persons of immense enthusiasm, passion and experimentation. And you have a garden of maturity, too. Old roses and herbaceous borders sit well beside the walled kitchen/ flower garden. You may purchase plants from their important plant collections. Open daily Feb-Oct 10-7. 01285 831300 (92/B5) cerneygardens.com

Kiftsgate Court Garden. Rare shrubs, plants, and an exceptional collection of roses in a magnificent situation. Water Garden. Plants for sale. Open Days. Open Apr & Sept Su, M & W 2-6. May-July Sa-W 12-6, Aug Sa-W 2-6. 01386 438777 (105/J6) kiftsgate.co.uk

Little Malvern Court & Gardens. Former Benedictine monastery. Home of the Russell and Berington families since the Dissolution. Priors Hall with needlework, family and European furniture and paintings. 10-acre garden; spring bulbs, rose garden and views. Open mid-Apr to mid-July W & Th only 2.15-5. 01684 892988 (102/A8) littlemalverncourt.co.uk

Bourton House Garden

Kiftsgate Court Garden ss

Mill Dene Garden, Blockley.

A beautiful 2 1/2-acres set around an historic water mill. Rose terrace, grotto and trout stream. Lunches and teas. Open Apr-Sept, W-Su from 10, except in July. 01386 70045 (99/J1) milldenegarden.co.uk

Misarden Park Gardens. One

of the most romantic gardens in England and home of the Wills family has shrubs, a traditional rose garden, perennial borders, extensive yew topiary, magnolia Goulangeana and spring bulbs amidst a picturesque woodland setting. Rill and Summerhouse. The Elizabethan mansion has mullion windows and was extended by Waterhouses in the C19 and by Lutyens who added a new wing between 1920-21. The gardens are open all year Tu-Su & BHs 10-5. Nursery with Garden Café and Pop-Up Restaurant awaits your taste buds is open daily except M. 01285 821303 (91/K5) misardenpark.co.uk

Painswick Rococo Garden.

A beautiful C18 Rococo garden in 6-acres dating from a period of flamboyant and romantic garden design nestles in a hidden Cotswold valley. Be sure you visit in February for the display of magical snowdrops. Open daily mid-Jan to Oct, 11-5. Restaurant and Gift Shop. 01452 81320 (90/F4)

Westonbirt Arboretum. If you

believe trees to be the most beautiful things in creation then a visit to this wonderland must be at the top of your agenda. Here, in this arboreal paradise garden you will find 600-acres of magnificent trees and shrubs from around the world. With no less than 15,500 individual specimens of 3,000 different tree types and a good 17-miles of footpaths ahead, you will need comfy footwear. Needless to say, it is quite a sight in spring and autumn, and popular too. Oak Hall Visitor Centre, gift shop and courtyard café. Plant centre. Open daily 9-dusk, from 8 at W/Es. 01666 880220 (88/E5) forestry.gov.uk/westonbirt

Bibury Trout Farm

Arlingham, St Augustine's Farm. Working farm where you can explore the 50 organic acres, stroke and feed the animals, and buy free range eggs. Open Mar to Oct Tu-Su 11 5. 01452 740277 (87/C3) staugustinesfarm.co.uk

Bibury Trout Farm. This working trout farm lies in a beautiful setting beside the River Coln. You can feed the fish, or try your hand at fly fishing in the Beginner's Fishery (hours vary). There are fresh and prepared trout on sale, as well as plants and shrubs. Gift shop. Light refreshments. Open summer M-Sa 8-6, Su 10-6, winter daily 8-4. 01285 740215 (93/G5) biburytroutfarm.co.uk

Cogges Manor Farm Museum, Church Lane, Witney. Historic buildings, exhibitions, traditional breeds of animals, daily demos and special weekends. *Downton Abbey* location. Garden, orchard and riverside walk. Café. Open mid-Mar to Oct Tu-F & BH Ms 10.30-5.30, W/Es 12-5.30. 01993 772602 (95/G4) cogges.org.uk

Cotswold Farm Park, Nr Bourton-On-the-Water. A unique survival centre for rare historic breeds of British farm animals including the Cotswold Lions (the Golden Fleece), is elevated high on the Central Wolds, three miles from Bourton. Pets and tots corner. Farm trail. Lambing, shearing and seasonal exhibitions. Café. Camp Site. Open daily, all year 10.30-5. 01451 850307 (98/F5) cotswoldfarmpark.co.uk

Bourton-On-The-Water, Santhill Fisheries. Mature 26-acre lake stocked with Rainbow and Brown Trout. Day, half-day, evening tickets and boat hire. Open Mar to 21 Dec. 01451 810291 These are flooded gravel pits from the 1960s and 70s. Now used for a carp farm, windsurfing centre and angling lake. There is a great abundance of wildlife: plants, insects and birds. (99/K8)

John Moore Countryside Museum, 41 Church Street, Tewkesbury. Dedicated to children and all aspects of nature conservation displayed in a C15 timber framed house. John Moore lived below Bredon Hill and wrote novels about the English Countryside most notably his *Brensham Trilogy*. His books are currently out of fashion but need reviving! Open Apr to Oct Tu-Sa & BHs, 10-1 & 2-5. 01684 297174 (101/H2)

Cogges Manor Farm Museum

Lloyd Baker Countryside Collection, The Old Prison, Northleach. Fascinating medley of agricultural implements: carts and bygone machinery. Café. Open Apr-Oct W-Sa 11-4. (92/F1)

South Cerney, Cotswold Water Park. This covers an area of 40-square miles of countryside and is split into three sections: the Western section, the Keynes Country Park and the Eastern Section (near Fairford). There are 140 lakes, 74 fishing lakes, 10 lakes with SSSI status, 40 different lake owners and 150km of pathways, bridleways and cycleways. 20,000 people live in the park's 14 main settlements. The extraction of the gravel and sand deposits from the 'catchment area' of the Upper Thames left large holes that were in 1967 designated to become a water park. From its humble beginnings at the South Cerney Sailing Club the park now attracts more than half-a-million visitors a year. Children love the sandy beach and sculptures at Keynes whilst the more active are beckoned to the wake boarding and slalom skis at WM Ski on Spine Road wmski.com. A visit to the Gateway Centre on Spine Road is recommended before you explore the park where you can eat and drink at the Coot's Café daily from 9-5. Just opposite is the retailer Cotswold Outdoor for all your walking and camping supplies. Further down the road overlooking Spring Lake, the Lakeside Brasserie for coffees, beers, pizzas, burgers and children's meals. (92/D10) watermarkclub.co.uk

St James City Farm. Albany St, Tredworth. Hands-on contact with farm animals, some rare breeds. Picnic and play areas. Open all year, M-Sa 9.30-4.30. 01452 305728 (90/E1)

Thistledown Farm, Nympsfield. Promotes the awareness of agricultural and environmental practices by tackling ecological issues head on in a fun way. Follow the adventure, sculpture and wildlife trails. Organic campsite. Café open W-Su 9-4.30 all year. 01453 860420 (90/C8) thistledown.org.uk

FARM SHOPS & EATERIES

Butts Farm (& Farm Shop), South Cerney. Rare breeds, sheep, fowl, pigs and cattle in 30-acres of meadowland. Tractor safari. Picnics. Pets corner. Open Apr-Sept Tu-Sa & BHs (daily in hols & winter Su) 9-6. 01285 862224 (92/D9) buttsfarmrarebreeds.co.uk

Chedworth Farm Shop, Denfurlong Farm. If you seek fresh produce, none better; a butchery, café, dairy, fruit and veg, ice cream, fish and chips, and a camping site. Open daily from 9. 01285 720265 (92/D4) chedworthfarmshop.co.uk

Cotswold Food Store & Café, Longborough. The husband and wife team of Bernard and Joanne champion local produce; local pies, cheeses, deli salads, homemade cakes and quiches, and the cafés produces a full English breakfast, as well as vegetarian dishes. Open daily except Monday from 9, and Sundays from 10. 01451 830469 (99/J4) cotswoldfoodstore.com

Daylesford Organic Farm Shop. The doyen of farm shops that takes the Harrods experience onto a sward of English turf. On display are the fine foods direct from their 2,350 acres of organic fields and pastures. Kitchen and bakery. Café. Accommodation in Cottages and Bamford Haybarn Spa. Cookery School on 01608 731620. Open daily M-Sa 9-6, Su 10-4. 01608 731700 (96/A5) daylesford.com

Organic Farm Shop, Burford Road, Cirencester. A working farm and eco destination that has it all: café/restaurant, camping, eco-venue and courses, corporate and wedding functions, and a vegetable garden. Open from 9 Tu-Sa, (Su from 11). 01285 640441 (92/C7) theorganicfarmshop.co.uk

Gloucester Services (M5) Farm Shop & Café. Why can't all motorway services be like this? It's a disgrace that the British public have had to put up with the filthy, unkempt and ill thought out services on our roads. Here at Gloucester the Westmorland Family have created an oasis of brilliant farm produce sourced from small local producers. There is a butchery, a deli and a café/restaurant. Indeed, you could be forgiven for thinking you have arrived in a *Hobbit's* village. So, where is *Bilbo Baggins*? Main Building opens at 6am to close at 10pm The Filling Station + Deli is open 24 hours. 01452 813254 (90/E2) gloucesterservices.com

Vegetable Matters ss

Cotswold Lions, Cotswold Farm Park

Hayles Fruit Farm. Wide range of locally produced fruit, cider and home-cured hams. Orchard Tea room open daily 9-5. Two nature trails. Camping. Open daily. 01242 602123 (98/D4) haylesfruitfarm.co.uk

Jesse Smith Farm Shop, Café & Deli, 13A, 19 Love Lane, Cirencester. Cotswold (& Cirencester) carnivores have known six generations of Smiths provide them with high-quality mouth-watering butchered meat - since time began. The Smiths have associations with Cotswold farmers who are fanatical about their livestock. The success of this business has been in the detail; the husbandry, the craftsmanship and workmanship. Open from 8-6 Monday to Friday, Saturday 8-5, Sunday 10-4. The Kitchen opens until 3 pm, Sunday lunch from midday. 01285 653352 (92/B8) jessesmith.co.uk

Upton Firehouse & Farm Shop Burford. Their smoked meats, game and fish are well-known, as is their shop selling British, Italian and Spanish goodies. The Firehouse can BBQ enormous pieces of meat for family parties seated at long trestle tables. Licensed bar. Open M-Sa 10-5.30, Su 11-3. Burford Market (50 stalls) on Sa 10-4. 01993 823699 (93/M3) uptonsmokery.co.uk

Vegetable Matters Farm Shop & Café, May Lane, Ebrington. As the name suggests, vegetables (boxes) are the speciality. As well as fresh flowers and seasonal fruit. Café for light lunches and coffees who welcome walkers, cyclists and passers-by (horses riders, too). Open from 8.30 Tuesday to Saturday, Sunday from 10. 01386 593326 (105/K8) vegetablematters.co.uk

You May Also Like to Consider:

Wyatts Plant Centre & Farm Shop, Great Rollright. Ice cream and farm shop in organic conversion. "Rose" specialist. Garden nursery, restaurant, animals and play area. Open daily 9-5.30. 01608 684835 (96/D2)

Cotswold Falcony Centre

Birdland Park & Gardens, Bourton. Bird garden on banks of the pretty River Windrush. Penguins, tropical and sub-tropical birds. Open daily, Apr-Oct 10-5, Nov-Mar 10-4. 01451 820480 (99/K8) birdland.co.uk

Cattle Country Adventure Park, Berkeley. Gone are the bison, now very much fun goings-on like ferret racing. Play area. Pets corner. Open daily East-Oct 10-5. 01453 810510 (108/C9) cattlecountry.co.uk

Cotswold Falconry Centre, Batsford Park. The Centre is dedicated to the conservation of eagles, hawks, falcons and owls, with many breeding pairs. Flying displays throughout the day. New Parliament of Owls. Open daily mid-Feb to mid-Nov 10.30-5. 01386 701043 (99/C9) cotswold-falconry.co.uk

Cotswold Wildlife Park, Nr Burford. Animals, birds and reptiles from all corners of the globe, beautifully laid out in 120-acres of gardens and parkland. Adventure playground. Tropical House. Children's farmyard. Facilities for the disabled. Picnic area. Café. Open daily from 10. 01993 823006 (94/A5) cotswoldwildlifepark.co.uk

Elver Fishing. The elver, a baby eel arrives here in Spring after a two year journey from the Sargasso Sea. Fished with nets at Epney on the Severn they are considered a culinary delicacy (if par-boiled and fried in bacon fat),

White Rhinos, Cotswold Wildlife Park ss

Shore Humboldts & King Penguins, Birdland ss

and reputed to be aphrodisiac. Elvers mature in isolated ponds, then return across the Atlantic to spawn. (90/A3)

Gloucestershire Wildlife Trust, Robinswood Hill Country Park. Visitor Centre, exhibition and gift shop. Open daily 9-5, W/Es 11-4.30. 01452 383333 (90/E2) gloucestershirewildlifetrust.co.uk

Prinknash Bird & Deer Park. Collection of over 50 wildfowl, waterfowl and tame deer. New Visitor Centre & Café. Open daily 10-5 (-4.30 in winter). 01452 812727 (91/G2) thebirdpark.com

Waterfowl Sanctuary & Children's Farm. Rare breeds and hands-on children's farm with friendly animals. Baby Barn. Open Tu-Su 10.30-5 (dusk if earlier). 01608 730252 (97/H1) waterfowlsanctuary.co.uk

Wildfowl & Wetlands Trust, Slimbridge. Founded by the late Sir Peter Scott in 1946; home of the world's largest collection of flamingos, swans, geese and ducks - over 2,500 wildfowl. Restaurant, Shop, Picnic areas, Free wheelchairs for disabled. Open daily; summer 9.30-5.30, winter 9.30-5. 01453 891900 (108/C7) wwt.org.uk

Flamingos, Wildfowl & Wetlands Trust

Bourton Lakes. These are flooded gravel pits from the 1960s and 70s. Now used for a carp farm, windsurfing centre and angling lake. There is a great abundance of wildlife: plants, insects and birds. (99/K8)

Broadway Tower Country Park. A unique Cotswold attraction: an C18 folly tower with historical and geographical exhibitions. Country retreat of the pre-Raphaelite, William Morris. Breeders of red deer with adventure playground, nature walks, fab café and gift shops. Nuclear Bunker Days. Superb views from the top of the Tower – a clear day gives a view of 12 counties. Open daily all year: Café 9-5, Tower 10-5, NB 10-4.45 W/ Es & BHS. 01386 852390 (104/F10) broadwaytower.co.uk

Churn Valley. A memorable route from Seven Springs to Cirencester follows one of England's most scenic drives. The variety of the trees and the sunken river valley are a sight to behold. Beware, this is a fast road and accidents are frequent. (92/B3)

Cirencester Park. Belongs to the Bathurst family who have generously opened their grounds for many years giving you the opportunity to walk in 3,000 acres of landscaped parkland, and along a five-mile avenue of horse chestnuts and hardwoods that were planted in the early C18. The C18 mansion is home to Lord Apsley and is not open to the general public. If you like hobnobbing with celebrities you have the opportunity to do so by watching polo on most Sundays at 3pm, from May to September, see website or 01285 640410. The park opens daily all year from 8-5. Separate entrance to the Cricket and Tennis clubs on the Stroud road. (92/B8) cirencesterpark.co.uk

Croome Park, Nr Pershore. 'Capability' Brown's first significant landscape project. A restoration plan has begun - dredging and replanting the Lake Garden. Open Mar,Sept & Oct W-Su, daily Apr to Aug, Xmas & Jan W/ Es, 11-5. 01905 371006 (103/G6) nationaltrust.org.uk

Devil's Chimney, Leckhampton. A 50 foot high limestone rock which according to local superstition 'rises from hell.' Its origins resulted from quarrying the surrounding stone. (101/K9)

Coln Valley. Charming valley with typically quaint Cotswold villages: Ablington, Calcot, Coln Rogers, Coln St Dennis, and Winson. (92/F4)

Broadway Tower Country Park

Sherborne Brook in Frost

Golden Valley. Runs from Sapperton to Chalford and is especially fine with the arrival of the Autumnal colours of beech, ash and oak. (91/J7)

Highnam Woods Nature Reserve. 300-acres of broad-leafed woodland with bluebells in spring. Nightingales call (if you are listening). Open daily. 01594 562852 (100/B9) rspb.org.uk

Leckhampton Hill. A popular dog walking area for Cheltonians providing superb views towards the Malvern Hills and Wales. The golden stone of 'Regency' Cheltenham was quarried here. Iron Age and Roman camps. (101/K9)

You May Also Like to Consider:

Macaroni Downs, Eastleach. Quite a sight. These rolling sheep pastures were once the location for Regency derring-do, gambling and horse racing. Now just munched by sheep. (93/K6)

Seven Springs, Coberley. One of the Sources of the River Thames. There is a stone plaque here with a Latin inscription which reads, roughly translated: *'Here thou, O Father Thames, hast thy sevenfold beginning'.* (101/L10)

Sherborne Park Estate (NT). Waymarked walks through woods and parkland with fine views. (93/J2) nationaltrust.org.uk

The Bottoms; Waterley Bottom, Tyley Bottom and Ozleworth Bottom. Deep combes (valleys) of rare and solitary beauty rich in wild flowers and bird life. And all can be viewed from countless footpaths. Strange to believe but in the C17 and C18 Waterley operated 15 fulling mills (to cleanse and thicken cloth) within a radius of 5-miles. (88/A2))

Windrush Valley. A slow, trickling stream in summer with a tendency to flood in winter. The river snakes its way through quiet golden villages, creating the idyllic Cotswold scene. (93/K1)

Devil's Chimney, Leckhampton

Cam Long Down

Chalford Valley Nature Trail. Passes beside the River Frome and the Thames & Severn Canal. Parking near Round House by the Industrial Estate. (91/H7)

Chedworth Woods. A network of footpaths that criss-cross through tangled woodland close to the Roman Villa. (92/C2)

Coombe Hill Canal Nature Reserve. Two-mile stretch of canal closed in 1876. Habitat of birds, dragonflies, aquatic and bankside plants. Open all year. (100/F5)

Cooper's Hill, Nr Brockworth. 137-acres of common land in which to roam wild criss-crossed by nature trails. Start from the car park at Fiddler's Elbow. The scene of the Cheese-Rolling ceremony on Whit Monday at 6pm – a large cheese (originally representing the Sun in a Pagan ceremony) is chased down the hill. Only for the fittest and craziest at heart for limbs have known to be fractured here on many occasions. Scene of an Iron Age fort. (91/G2)

Cranham Woods. Bluebells and white garlic bloom in Spring, and a web of footpaths are spread throughout this tangled woodland. Best approached from Birdlip in early summer when the foliage is green and new. (91/H3)

Ebworth Estate, Sheepscombe. Woodland walks through beech woods Rich in wildlife managed by English Nature. No parking facilities. 01452 814213 (91/H3)

Fish Hill Woods, Broadway Hill. Attractive woodland providing superb views. (105/G9)

Minchinhampton Common. A wide open space popular with dog walkers, horse riding, golfers and the ancient Saxons final resting place - see the Long Barrows and Earthworks. (90/F8)

Rodborough Common. 800 acres of open space provides great walks and views across the Stroud Valleys. (90/E7)

Wychwood Forest, Charlbury. Formerly a Royal Hunting forest. The around Cornbury Park is richly wooded and makes for a fine 9-mile circular walk. Start beside the Bull in Charlbury. (96/F9)

A long distance footpath covering 97-miles, from Chipping Campden to Bath. It follows the edge of the escarpment, meanders through picturesque villages past pre-historic sites and provides spectacular views. It is waymarked.

Brackenbury Ditches, North Nibley. This is an impregnable Iron Age fort and a splendid viewpoint with views across the Severn Vale and Welsh Mountains. Worth the walk around to the Tyndale Monument. (108/E3)

Broadway Tower. Starting from the Tower you can make a circular walk of 2.5 miles to Broadway and back. (104/F10)

Cam Long Down, Nr Cam. A humpbacked ridge of oolitic limestone that once seen is never forgotten. From the top it's a good viewpoint surrounded by beech woods and bracken. (90/A9)

Cleeve Hill. At 1,083 feet this is the highest point in the Cotswolds and thus a superb viewpoint across to the Malvern Hills, Welsh Mountains and northwards across the Cotswold landscape. A popular dog walking area and in winter snow ideal for tobaggan runs. In 1901 a tramway was built from Cheltenham to Cleeve Cloud but sadly closed in 1930. Cleeve Cloud is the site of an Iron Age hill fort and just below the scarp is The Ring a site of religious/pagan rituals 100 feet in diameter. Castle Rock is popular with novice rock climbers. (101/M5)

Cleeve Common. A vast expanse of common land where you are free to roam with dog and friends. It is more like a piece of wild moorland with its extensive horizons and you may be forgiven for believing you are in the midst of a National Park. There are wild flowers, the Gallops (for exercising race horses) and tracks that lead off in all directions. Park in the golf course or in the lay-byes on the B4632. (101/M5)

Crickley Hill Country Park. Nature trails, geological and archaeological trails are signposted, as is the Cotswold Way. There are traces of Stone Age and Iron Age settlements. Fine views. Open daily. (91/J1)

Coaley Peak. On the edge of the Cotswold escarpment affording fine views. Picnic area. Ice Cream van. (90/B8)

Dover's Hill. A natural amphitheatre on a spur of the Cotswolds with magnificent views over the Vale of Evesham. The 'Olympick Games & Scuttlebrook Wake' have been held here since 1612 and take place the Friday and Saturday following the Spring Bank Holiday. (105/G8)

Frocester Hill. A superb viewpoint rising to 778 feet provides superb views over the Severn Estuary, Welsh Hills and Forest of Dean. (90/C8)

Haresfield Beacon & Standish Wood (NT). High open grassland at 700 feet that was a natural fort held by Iron Age and Roman settlements. Delightful when the bluebells and primroses bloom in the Spring. (90/D5)

Bull in Field, Coln Valley

Banbury, Oxford Canal. Built by James Brindley in 1769 to connect the industrial Midlands with London via the River Thames. Financial problems delayed the construction but it was eventually to reach Oxford in 1789. Today, it runs for 77 miles from Hawkesbury Junction, south of Coventry to Oxford. You can enjoy a multitude of leisure activities, from solitary walks to boating, canoeing, cycling, fishing and the wildlife. (107/M8) waterscape.com

Banbury, Tooley's Boatyard & Tours, Spiceball Park Road. This is the oldest working dry dock boatyard on the inland waterways of Britain. Established in 1790 to build and repair the wooden horse-drawn narrow boats. 200-year old forge, chandlery and gift shop. Self drive hire and private boat trips. 01295 272917 (107/M7) tooleysboatyard.co.uk

Bourton Model Railway. Over 500 sq.ft. of exhibits. Continental trains and British Railway trains in HO/OO and N Gauge. Open June/Aug daily 11-5, Sept-May W/Es 11-5. 01451 820686 (99/J8) bourtonmodelrailway.co.uk

Bugatti Trust, Prescott Hill. A small exhibition illustrates the work of Ettore Bugatti genius of industrial design and invention. Study Centre with drawings, photos and some cars. Open M-F 10-4, (Nov-Feb M-Th) and during Hill Climb days. 01242 677201 (101/M4) bugatti-trust.co.uk

Chipping Campden, Harts Silversmiths - The Old Silk Mill. Founded in 1888 as part of the 'Arts & Crafts' movement. The Harts gold and silversmith workshop is the last operating remnant of the Guild of Handicraft which C R Ashbee established in 1888 and which moved to this village in 1902. Café. Open all year. 01386 841100 (105/H8) hartsilversmiths.co.uk

Classic Motor Hub, Bibury Airfield. This is more than just a car showroom, it's a motorist's dream destination in the heart of the Cotswolds. The Hub holds regular motoring events throughout the year and is open by prior arrangement on weekdays for those seeking a classic, vintage or high-performance car. They also offer car storage, a workshop and transportation services. 01242 384092 (93/G4) classicmotorhub.com

Cotswold Canals. The Stroudwater Navigation was opened in 1779, linking Stroud to the River Severn to serve the cloth industry of the Stroud Valleys. The Thames and Severn Canal was built to link the Stroudwater to the River Thames through the Sapperton Tunnel. The towpath is open and the best places to see the restored canal are at Eastington, near Stonehouse, both portals of the Sapperton Tunnel, and west of the Spine Road in the Cotswold Water Park. 01285 643440 (92/A5) cotswoldcanals.com

Cotswold Motoring Museum, Bourton. Motorcycles (including a Brough Superior) and vintage racing cars in C18 water mill. Collection of old advertising signs and toys. Open daily mid-Feb to mid-Dec 10-6. 01451 821255 (99/K8) cotswoldmotoringmuseum.co.uk

Donnington Brewery. Established in 1865 by Thomas Arkell who used the spring water to concoct his delicious potions. The brewery remains independent and supplies 15 tied houses and a number of free trade outlets. (101/J4) donnington-brewery.com

Filkins, Cotswold Woollen Weavers. A visit here is a "Must" for all who wish to learn about the Cotswolds; the story of wool and woollen cloth has woven its way into every fabric of Cotswold life, as has the stone that built the barns, churches and villages. The stone is displayed by the masons' sculptures and workmanship. The cloth, and the garments made up in their many guises (scarves, throws, jackets, as well as rolls of cloth) mirror the eccentricities of this unique establishment. Large mill shop & interiors gallery. Coffee shop. Picnic area. Masonry yard. Open daily M-Sa 10-6, Su 2-6. 01367 860491 (94/A7) cotswoldwollenweavers.co.uk

Gloucester & Sharpness Canal. Opened in 1827 and built above the River Severn. It's 16 miles long and was originally used by ocean-going ships in transit to Gloucester. Visitor Centres at Wallbridge Lock, open M-Sa from 10 and Saul Junction, open W/Es 12.30-4. (85/A6)

Gloucester Waterways Museum, Llanthony Warehouse. A major national exhibition about the history of the inland waterways with major new refurbishments. Historic boats and Leisure Cruises Café. Open daily 11-4. July-Aug 10.30-5. 01452 318200 (100/D9) gloucesterwaterwaysmuseum.org.uk

Hook Norton Brewery. Visitor Centre displays brewing artefacts from 1849 to today. Open all year M-Sa & BHs, 9.30-4.30. Two-hour tours from 11. 01608 737210 (97/G2) hooky.co.uk

Jet Age Museum, Gloucester Airport. Collection of Gloucester built aircraft with artefacts representing the county's contribution to aviation. Frank Whittle Exhibition. Open W/Es & BHs. (101/G7) jetagemuseum.org

Morgan Motor Company, Spring Lane. Morgan is the iconic British sports car and in its 110-year history was family owned with a community of 5,000 owners. However, it has recently been taken over by an Italian venture capital group to develop the brand. You can take a factory tour on various Saturdays and during the week M-Th & F am. Pre-book on: (102/B5) morgan-motor.co.uk

North Gloucestershire Railway, Toddington. Steam hauled narrow-gauge railway and museum. Trains operate from East-Oct Su & BHs 12-5. Times vary – check to confirm. 01242 621405 (98/D2) toddington-narrow-gauge.co.uk

Stroud Mills: Dunkirk Mill Centre. A mill with machinery driven by the largest working water wheel in Gloucestershire. Displays on the finishing processes of fulling, teasel raising and cross cutting. Access is via the Cycle Track by Egypt Mill. Open Apr to Sept on odd W/Es 2-4. 01453 766273 (90/E9) stroud-textile.org.uk

Uley, The Old Brewery. The mill owner, Samuel Price built this brewery in 1833 to assuage his workers thirst. It was restored in 1984 and has since won many awards for their Old Spot, Pigs Ear and Uley Bitter. It is not open to prying visitors, only the trade. You can sample their wares in the Old Crown Inn at the top of the village, or in various hostelries around the Cotswolds. (88/B1)

Oxford Canal, Banbury

Old Mill Museum, Lower Slaughter

Compton Verney. Art Gallery in C18 Robert Adam mansion set in parkland by 'Capability' Brown; Naples School, British Portraits, Folk Art. Open mid-Mar to mid-Dec Tu-Su & BHs 10.30-5. 01926 645500 (106/D1) comptonverney.org.uk

Court Barn Museum, Chipping Campden. A celebration of the town's association with the *Arts & Crafts Movement*. An exhibition of silver, jewellery ceramics, sculpture, industrial design and more, all beautifully set up by the Guild of Handicraft Trust. Open Tu-Sa 10-5 & BH Ms (-4 Oct to Mar) (105/H8) courtbarn.org.uk

Corinium Museum, Cirencester. Impressive collection of Roman remains clearly displayed to relate the development of the Cotswolds from the earliest times with special reference to the Roman period. Open daily all year M-Sa 10-5, Su 2-5. Attached to Jack's Coffee Shop. 01285 655611 (92/B8) coriniummuseum.co.uk

Gloucester Life Museum, 99-103 Westgate St., Gloucester Medieval timber-framed buildings associated with martyrdom of Bishop Hooper in 1555. Social history, folklore, crafts and industries of city and county. Herb garden. Open Tu-Sa 10-5. 01452 396868 (100/E10) gloucester.gov.uk/folkmuseum

Gordon Russell Design Museum, 15 Russell Square, Broadway. A collection spanning 60-years that is dedicated to one of the C20s finest furniture designers. With original design drawings and furniture embracing the *Arts & Crafts Movement*. Open Tu-Su 11-4 & BH Ms. 01386 854695 (104/F9) gordonrussellmuseum.org

Gustav Holst Birthplace Museum, Clarence Road. Pittville. Cheltenham. Memorabilia of the composer's life. Period Furnished rooms. Open all year Tu-Sa 10-4, Su 1.30-5. Closed mid-Dec to Feb. 01242 524846 (101/K7) holstmuseum.org.uk

Jenner's Museum & Garden, Berkeley. A Queen Anne House with traditional and modern displays that celebrate the life of Edward Jenner, the surgeon who discovered a vaccine for smallpox. Open Apr to Sept, Tu-Sa 12.30-5.30, Su & BH Ms 1-5.30, & daily June to Aug, Oct Su 1-5.30. 01453 810631 (108/B9) jennermuseum.com

Museum In The Park, Stratford Park, Stroud. Innovative and colourful displays and changing exhibitions ranging from Dinosaurs to the Uley Roman Temple to the world's first lawnmower and contemporary sculpture. Open Apr to Sept Tu-F 10-5, W/Es & BHs 11-5. Oct to Mar Tu-F 10-4, W/Es 11-4. 01453 763394 (90/E6) museuminthepark.org.uk

Museum of Gloucester, Brunswick Road. Recently undergone a major restoration project; Roman relics, dinosaurs, aquarium, art exhibitions. Open Tu-Sa 10-5. 01452 396131 (100/D10) gloucester.gov.uk/citymuseum

Old Mill Museum, Lower Slaughter. This iconic C19 flour mill has been lovingly restored into a small museum with ice cream parlour, tea room and mill shop, all overlooking the Mill Leat (pond). The proprietor is the lead singer in a Jazz band, Hence, the funky music. Open daily (W/Es Jan to Feb), 10-6. 01451 820052 (99/J7) oldmill-lowerslaughter.com

Oxfordshire Museum, Park Street, Woodstock. An impressive and coherent exhibition of Oxfordshire and its people, from earliest times to the present day.

Changing exhibitions. Coffee shop. Open daily Tu-Sa 10-5, Su 2-5. 01993 811456 (97/L10) oxfordshire.gov.uk

You May Also Like to Consider:

The Wilson - Art Gallery & Museum, Clarence St., Cheltenham. A world-renowned *Arts & Crafts Movement* collection inspired by William Morris. Rare Chinese, and English ceramics. Social history of Cheltenham. C17 Dutch and C17-20 British paintings. Host to the Gloucestershire Guild of Craftsmen. Open daily 10-5 (-4 Nov-Mar). Closed BHs. 01242 237431 (101/K7) cheltenhammuseum.org.uk

World of Mechanical Music, Northleach. One of the finest attractions in the Cotswolds where you will always be met with a cheery welcome. An enchanting wonderland of mechanical musical instruments, clocks and restored musical boxes. 'Magical Musicals'. Café/Bar. Open daily 10-5. 01451 860181 (93/G2) mechanicalmusic.co.uk

Roman Figures, Corinium Museum

BUYING ART & CRAFTSMANSHIP

Brian Sinfield Gallery, 27 The Hill, Burford. Highly respected gallery featuring changing exhibitions of modern and contemporary paintings, sculpture and ceramics. Open Tu-Sa, 10-5. 01993 824464 (94/B3) briansinfield.com

Campden Gallery, High Street. One of the most respected of Cotswold galleries has constant changing exhibitions of paintings, sculpture and prints. Open daily Tu-Sa 10-5,30, Su 11-4. 01386 841555 (105/H8) campdengallery.co.uk

Fosse Gallery, The Square, Stow. Well-established gallery displaying paintings; contemporary and modern, most artists are RA, RAI, ROI members. Open Tu-Sa 10.30-5. 01451 831319 (99/K5) fossegallery.com

Iona House Gallery, Woodstock. Paintings, etchings, prints, sculpture, ceramics, glass, textiles, silver and wood. Open M-Sa 10-5.30, Su 11-5. 01993 811464 (97/L10) ionahousegallery.org

John Davies Gallery, The Old Dairy Plant, Moreton-in-Marsh. . A much respected Cotswold gallery established in 1977. Six fully catalogued annual exhibitions. Fine period, post

New Brewery Arts ss

Impressionist and contemporary paintings. Open M-Sa 9.30-5. 01608 652255 (99/M2) johndaviesgallery.com

New Brewery Arts, Brewery Court, Cirencester. A centre for excellence in contemporary arts and crafts with Exhibition Gallery, coffee house, crafts shop, theatre and resident craft workers. Open M-Sa 9-5, Su 10-4. 01285 657181 (92/B8) newbreweryarts.org.uk

Prema, Uley. Independent rural arts centre shows new work by emerging artists in their converted chapel. Open M-F. 01453 860703 (90/B10) prema.demon.co.uk

Red Rag Gallery, Church Street, Stow. Original paintings from living artists. Sculpture. Scottish art. Open M-Sa 10-5, Su 10-4. 01451 832563 (99/K6) redraggallery.co.uk

Richard Hagen Gallery, High St., Broadway. One of the Cotswold's finest galleries who specialise in contemporary artists: Stephen Mangan, Jean B Martin, Linda Styles...many awash with colour. Open daily except W & Su. 10-1, 2-5. 01386 853624 (104/F9) richardhagen.com

Wet Paint Gallery, London Road, Chalford. Colourful, abstract and modern landscapes, ceramics and glass. Open Tu-Sa 10-5. 01285 644990 (91/H8) contemporary-art-holdings.co.uk

Saied Dai, Brian Sinfield Gallery

Campden Gallery

Aston Pottery. Working from clay to finished, hand-stencilled pottery. Demonstrations, shop and café. Open M-Sa 9-5, Su 10.30-5. 01993 852031 (94/F7) astonpottery.co.uk

Beckford Silk. Hand printers of silk. Gallery of Textiles. Tours of factory. Coffee shop 10-4. Open M-Sa 9-5. 01386 881507 (103/L10) beckfordsilk.co.uk

Conderton Pottery. Distinctive stoneware pots by specialist salt glazed country potter, Toff Milway. Open M-Sa 9-5. 01386 725387 (103/L9) toffmilway.co.uk

Cotswold Pottery, Bourton. Traditional rustic pots, hand-thrown using local materials. Bronze sculptures too. Open M-Sa 10-4, Su 11-4. 01451 820173 (99/J8) cotswoldpottery.co.uk

Gallery Pangolin, Chalford. Specializes in modern and contemporary bronze sculptures that have been caste in their foundry, and also sculptures' drawings. Open M-F 10-6, Sa 10-1. 01453 886527 (91/G8) gallery-pangolin.com

Harts Silversmiths, Sheep St., Chipping Campden. The Harts gold and silversmith workshop is the last operating remnant of the Guild of Handicraft which C.R. Ashbee established in 1888 and which moved to Chipping Campden in 1902. Café. Open all year. 01386 841100 (105/H8) hartsilversmiths.co.uk

Lansdown Pottery, Stroud. A small group of potters work here developing their own different styles. It is also a centre or learning and art shows with the Studio, Glaze room, Kiln Room and extensive Library. Open M-F 10-5. 01453 753051 (90/E5) lansdownpottery.co.uk

Long Room Gallery, High St. Winchcombe. This is quite find and an unusual archival collection of Studio and Country Slipware from the C19 and C20, and a 'must-see" for all ceramic enthusiasts. Michael Cardew's pots on display. Open daily 100-501242 602319 (98/B3)

Whichford Pottery. Hand-made English terracotta flowerpots of immense size. Thirty craftsmen and women. Shop. Open daily M-F 9-5, Sa 10-4. 01608 684416 (96/D1) whichfordpottery.com

Winchcombe Pottery. One of the country's most respected potteries known throughout the ceramic world. A large variety of hand-made domestic ware on sale in the shop. Open daily M-F 8-5, Sa 10-4 (& Su Apr-Dec 11-4). 01242 602462 (98/B3) winchcombepottery.co.uk

Gallery Pengolin

BIBURY WALK

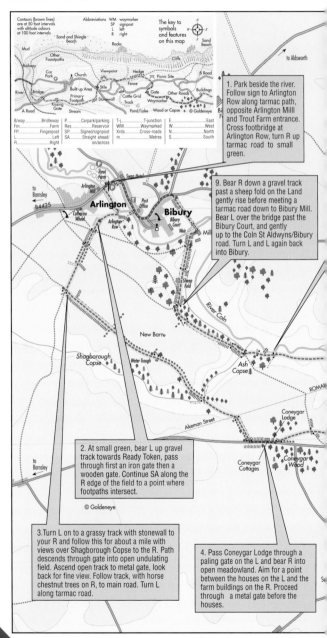

1. Park beside the river. Follow sign to Arlington Row along tarmac path, opposite Arlington Milll and Trout Farm entrance. Cross footbridge at Arlington Row, turn R up tarmac road to small green.

9. Bear R down a gravel track past a sheep fold on the Land gently rise before meeting a tarmac road down to Bibury Mill. Bear L over the bridge past the Bibury Court, and gently up to the Coln St Aldwyns/Bibury road. Turn L and L again back into Bibury.

2. At small green, bear L up gravel track towards Ready Token, pass through first an iron gate then a wooden gate. Continue SA along the R edge of the field to a point where footpaths intersect.

© Goldeneye

3. Turn L on to a grassy track with stonewall to your R and follow this for about a mile with views over Shagborough Copse to the R. Path descends through gate into open undulating field. Ascend open track to metal gate, look back for fine view. Follow track, with horse chestnut trees on R, to main road. Turn L along tarmac road.

4. Pass Coneygar Lodge through a paling gate on the L and bear R into open meadowland. Aim for a point between the houses on the L and the farm buildings on the R. Proceed through a metal gate before the houses.

This is one of the most popular walks in the Cotswolds for it is an easy walk along a pretty river valley connecting two enchanting villages. For those with tired legs or little time the map indicates a short cut. The route is undulating and provides views of rolling sheep pastures, an old Roman route (barely visible), trout streams and rich water meadows. The views down onto the village of Coln St Aldwyns are delightful.

Distance
5.75 miles/9.2km

Minimum Time
3 hours

Level of Difficulty
Easy

Terrain/Paths
Farm tracks, woodland, grass.

Landscape
Rolling farmland, sheep pastures, river valley.

Dogs
To be kept under control at all times. Sheep pastures along riverside.

Public Toilets
Bibury, opposite river.

Parking (P)
Bibury

Recommended Start/Finish
Bibury or Coln St Aldwyns.

Location
Bibury is between Cirencester and Burford on the B4425

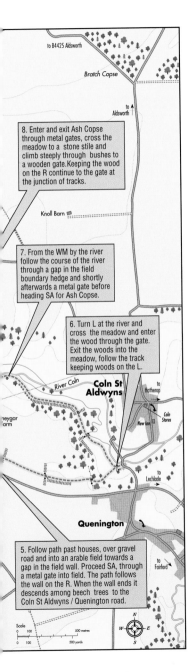

8. Enter and exit Ash Copse through metal gates, cross the meadow to a stone stile and climb steeply through bushes to a wooden gate. Keeping the wood on the R continue to the gate at the junction of tracks.

Knoll Barn

7. From the WM by the river follow the course of the river through a gap in the field boundary hedge and shortly afterwards a metal gate before heading SA for Ash Copse.

6. Turn L at the river and cross the meadow and enter the wood through the gate. Exit the woods into the meadow, follow the track keeping woods on the L.

River Coln

Coln St Aldwyns

5. Follow path past houses, over gravel road and into an arable field towards a gap in the field wall. Proceed SA, through a metal gate into field. The path follows the wall on the R. When the wall ends it descends among beech trees to the Coln St Aldwyns / Quenington road.

Quenington

Scale
0   100   500 metres
0   100   500 yards

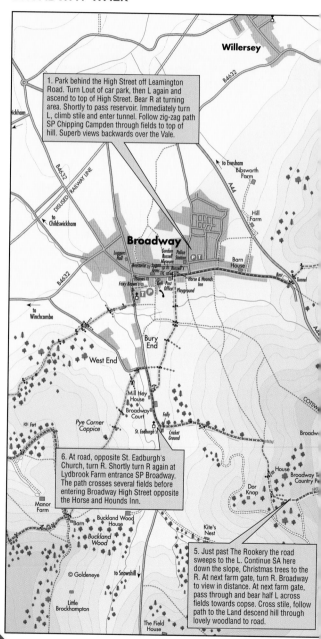

Willersey

1. Park behind the High Street off Leamington Road. Turn L out of car park, then L again and ascend to top of High Street. Bear R at turning area. Shortly to pass reservoir. Immediately turn L, climb stile and enter tunnel. Follow zig-zag path SP Chipping Campden through fields to top of hill. Superb views backwards over the Vale.

to Evesham

Bibsworth Farm

Hill Farm

Broadway

to Childswickham

Luggers Hall

Gordon Russell Museum

Police Station

Barn House

Lygon Arms TIC

Brasserie

Russell's

to Winchcombe

Thames Foxy Brown's

Bob Post Office

Horse & Hounds Inn

Playground

Bury End

West End

Mill Hay House

Broadway Court

Folly

COTSW

Broadw

Fort

Pye Corner Coppice

St. Eadburgh's

Cricket Ground

House

Broadway T Country Pa

6. At road, opposite St. Eadburgh's Church, turn R. Shortly turn R again at Lydbrook Farm entrance SP Broadway. The path crosses several fields before entering Broadway High Street opposite the Horse and Hounds Inn.

Dor Knap

Manor Farm

Barn

Buckland Wood House

Buckland Wood

Kite's Nest

© Goldeneye

to Snowshill

5. Just past The Rookery the road sweeps to the L. Continue SA here down the slope, Christmas trees to the R. At next farm gate, turn R. Broadway to view in distance. At next farm gate, pass through and bear half L across fields towards copse. Cross stile, follow path to the Land descend hill through lovely woodland to road.

Little Brockhampton

The Field House

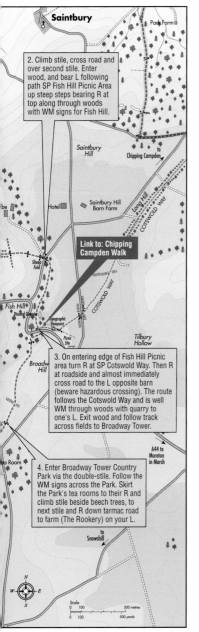

Saintbury

Parks Farm

2. Climb stile, cross road and over second stile. Enter wood, and bear L following path SP Fish Hill Picnic Area up steep steps bearing R at top along through woods with WM signs for Fish Hill.

Saintbury Hill

to Chipping Campden

Hotel

Saintbury Hill Barn Farm

Long Hill

COTSWOLD WAY

Link to: Chipping Campden Walk

COTSWOLD WAY

Sheep Fold

Fish Hill

Topographic Viewpoint

Picnic Site

Tilbury Hollow

Broadway Hill

3. On entering edge of Fish Hill Picnic area turn R at SP Cotswold Way. Then R at roadside and almost immediately cross road to the L opposite barn (beware hazardous crossing). The route follows the Cotswold Way and is well WM through woods with quarry to one's L. Exit wood and follow track across fields to Broadway Tower.

A44 to Moreton in Marsh

Tea Room

4. Enter Broadway Tower Country Park via the double-stile. Follow the WM signs across the Park. Skirt the Park's tea rooms to their R and climb stile beside beech trees, to next stile and R down tarmac road to farm (The Rookery) on your L.

to Snowshill

N
W — E
S

Scale
0   100   500 metres
0   100   500 yards

Broadway epitomises English domestic architecture at its finest, and so it is worth spending some time here before you venture forth out of the village up a relatively steep climb followed by a woodland walk and superb views over the vale. From Broadway Tower, it is possible, on a clear day, to see 13 counties. The descent is through a wood carpeted in wild flowers (bluebells in spring).

Distance
4.5 miles/7.2km

Minimum Time
3 hours

Grade/Level of Difficulty
Easy/Moderate

Terrain/Paths
Grass, farm tracks, paths.

Landscape
Rolling countryside, woodland.

Dogs
Fairly good for dogs - can run free in woodland. Keep under control around livestock.

Public Toilets
Broadway P & Broadway Tower Country Park.

Parking (P)
Broadway - behind High Street. There are two car parks in the village.

Recommended Start/Finish
Broadway P

Location
Broadway lies off the A44 midway between Evesham and Stow on the Wold, or on the B4632 midway between Cheltenham and Stratford upon Avon.

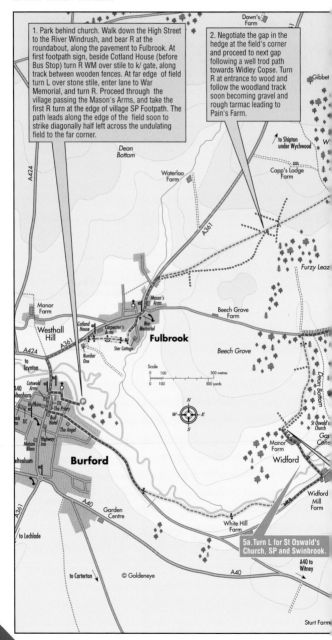

1. Park behind church. Walk down the High Street to the River Windrush, and bear R at the roundabout, along the pavement to Fulbrook. At first footpath sign, beside Cotland House (before Bus Stop) turn R WM over stile to k/ gate, along track between wooden fences. At far edge of field turn L over stone stile, enter lane to War Memorial, and turn R. Proceed through the village passing the Mason's Arms, and take the first R turn at the edge of village SP Footpath. The path leads along the edge of the field soon to strike diagonally half left across the undulating field to the far corner.

2. Negotiate the gap in the hedge at the field's corner and proceed to next gap following a well trod path towards Widley Copse. Turn R at entrance to wood and follow the woodland track soon becoming gravel and rough tarmac leading to Pain's Farm.

5a. Turn L for St Oswald's Church, SP and Swinbrook.

© Goldeneye

This is an easy, relaxing stroll away from the hustle and bustle of Burford. First, there is a slight ascent across open fields providing fine views of the surrounding countryside. Then, the route goes past conserved woodland to meander amidst lush green meadows beside the crystal clear waters of the River Windrush.

Distance
5.5 miles/8.8km

Minimum Time
2.5 hours

Grade/Level of Difficulty
Easy

Terrain/Paths
Grass, meadowland, farm tracks.

Landscape
Rolling pastureland, meadows in river valley.

Dogs
Popular dog walking spot along the river. Some livestock, however, mostly arable pastures. Dogs to be kept under control around livestock.

Public Toilets
Burford High Street

Parking (P)
Behind church, across bridge.

Recommended Start/ Finish Burford High Street

Location
On the A40 midway between Oxford and Cheltenham, or on the A361 eleven miles north of Lechlade.

---

3. Just beyond Pain's Farm the road sweeps L, turn R here SP Right of Way up farm track between stone walls. SA through gate towards wood (Faws Grove). Follow path as it bears away down to the three gates. The path leads up track between high hedges to road.

South Lodge

to Shipton under Wychwood

Faws Grove

Pain's Farm

Hit or Miss

to Fordwells

Handley Plain

4. Turn R at road junction. Walk along tarmac road until it dips down to edge of wood. Take the second footpath on your L SP Bridleway/ Widford half mile and enter a Game/Wildlife Conservation Area. The path follows the edge of the wood to the entrance to Manor Farm.

Swinbrook

to Asthall Leigh

Wildlife on Area

The Swan Inn

Cricket Ground

5. At the corner of field the path bears L WM descending to Manor Farm and through the farm yard down to the River Windrush along the tarmac road. Turn R at road junction, to shortly turn Rover stile WM Footpath, and continue to follow the course of the riverbank until you meet the road which leads to Burford.

Asthall

The Maytime

to A40 Burford and Witney

CHIPPING CAMPDEN WALK

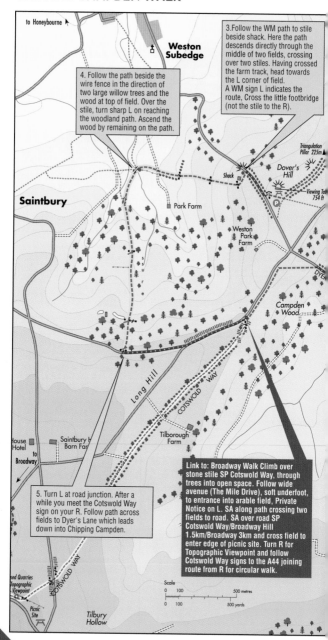

to Honeybourne ▶

Weston Subedge

Saintbury

3. Follow the WM path to stile beside shack. Here the path descends directly through the middle of two fields, crossing over two stiles. Having crossed the farm track, head towards the L corner of field. A WM sign L indicates the route, Cross the little footbridge (not the stile to the R).

4. Follow the path beside the wire fence in the direction of two large willow trees and the wood at top of field. Over the stile, turn sharp L on reaching the woodland path. Ascend the wood by remaining on the path.

Triangulation Pillar 225m▲

Dover's Hill

Shack

Viewing Table 754 ft

Park Farm

Weston Park Farm

SUFOLD

Campden Wood

DYER

Long Hill

COTSWOLD WAY

Tilborough Farm

House Hotel

Saintbury Barn Farm

to Broadway

5. Turn L at road junction. After a while you meet the Cotswold Way sign on your R. Follow path across fields to Dyer's Lane which leads down into Chipping Campden.

Link to: Broadway Walk Climb over stone stile SP Cotswold Way, through trees into open space. Follow wide avenue (The Mile Drive), soft underfoot, to entrance into arable field, Private Notice on L. SA along path crossing two fields to road. SA over road SP Cotswold Way/Broadway Hill 1.5km/Broadway 3km and cross field to enter edge of picnic site. Turn R for Topographic Viewpoint and follow Cotswold Way signs to the A44 joining route from R for circular walk.

sed Quarries Topographic Viewpoint

COTSWOLD WAY

Picnic Site

Tilbury Hollow

Scale
0   100   500 metres
0   100   500 yards

The route picks up the start of the Cotswold Way in Chipping Campden and follows it up to Dover's Hill, scene of the Cotswold Olympick Games. It then follows the edge of the Scarp to provide splendid views over the Vale of Evesham, before climbing up through enchanting woodland and then descending back into Chipping Campden.

Distance
4.25 miles/6.8km

Minimum Time
3 hours

Grade/Level of Difficulty
Easy/Moderate

Terrain/Paths
Tarmac, stone tracks, woodland paths.

Landscape
Arable fields, woodland and sheep pastures.

Dogs
Keep under control - beware livestock. Short section along road has grass verges.

Public Toilets
Chipping Campden High Street

Parking (P)
Beside Market Hall or at Dover's Hill P.

Recommended Start/ Finish Market Hall, Chipping Campden or Dover's Hill.

Location
On the B4081, off the A44 Broadway to Moreton in Marsh road.

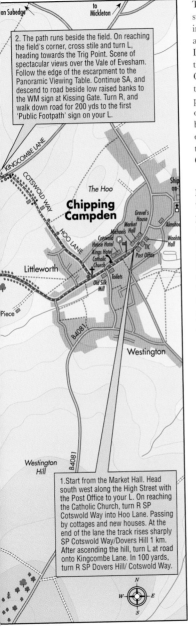

2. The path runs beside the field. On reaching the field's corner, cross stile and turn L, heading towards the Trig Point. Scene of spectacular views over the Vale of Evesham. Follow the edge of the escarpment to the Panoramic Viewing Table. Continue SA, and descend to road beside low raised banks to the WM sign at Kissing Gate. Turn R, and walk down road for 200 yds to the first 'Public Footpath' sign on your L.

1. Start from the Market Hall. Head south west along the High Street with the Post Office to your L. On reaching the Catholic Church, turn R SP Cotswold Way into Hoo Lane. Passing by cottages and new houses. At the end of the lane the track rises sharply SP Cotswold Way/Dovers Hill 1 km. After ascending the hill, turn L at road onto Kingcombe Lane. In 100 yards, turn R SP Dovers Hill/ Cotswold Way.

CLEEVE HILL WALK

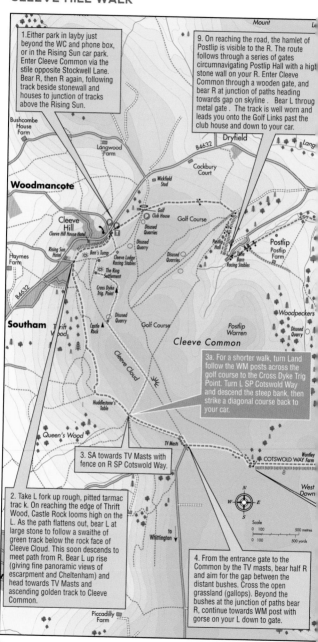

1. Either park in layby just beyond the WC and phone box, or in the Rising Sun car park. Enter Cleeve Common via the stile opposite Stockwell Lane. Bear R, then R again, following track beside stonewall and houses to junction of tracks above the Rising Sun.

9. On reaching the road, the hamlet of Postlip is visible to the R. The route follows through a series of gates circumnavigating Postlip Hall with a high stone wall on your R. Enter Cleeve Common through a wooden gate, and bear R at junction of paths heading towards gap on skyline . Bear L through metal gate . The track is well worn and leads you onto the Golf Links past the club house and down to your car.

3a. For a shorter walk, turn L and follow the WM posts across the golf course to the Cross Dyke Trig Point. Turn L SP Cotswold Way and descend the steep bank, then strike a diagonal course back to your car.

3. SA towards TV Masts with fence on R SP Cotswold Way.

2. Take L fork up rough, pitted tarmac trac k. On reaching the edge of Thrift Wood, Castle Rock looms high on the L. As the path flattens out, bear L at large stone to follow a swaithe of green track below the rock face of Cleeve Cloud. This soon descends to meet path from R. Bear L up rise (giving fine panoramic views of escarpment and Cheltenham) and head towards TV Masts and ascending golden track to Cleeve Common.

4. From the entrance gate to the Common by the TV masts, bear half R and aim for the gap between the distant bushes. Cross the open grassland (gallops). Beyond the bushes at the junction of paths bear R, continue towards WM post with gorse on your L down to gate.

Bushcombe House Farm
Langwood Farm
Woodmancote
Cleeve Hill
Cleeve Hill House Hotel
Haymes Farm
Rising Sun Hotel
Southam
Thrift Wood
Castle Rock
Queen's Wood
Piccadilly Farm

Mount
Dryfield
B4632
Cockbury Court
Wickfield Stud
Golf Club House
Golf Course
Disused Quarries
Disused Quarry
Ben's Tump
Cleeve Lodge Racing Stables
The Ring Settlement
Cross Dyke Trig. Point
Disused Quarry
Golf Course
Cleeve Cloud
Huddlestone's Table
TV Masts
to Whittington

Lang
Postlip
Postlip Hall
Postlip Farm
Tithe Barn Racing Stables
Woodpeckers
Postlip Warren
Disused Quarry
Cleeve Common
Wontley Farm
COTSWOLD WAY
West Down

Scale
0 100 500 metres
0 100 500 yards

W N E S

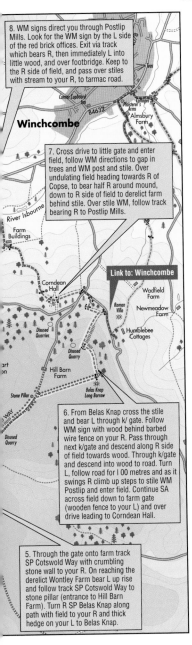

8. WM signs direct you through Postlip Mills. Look for the WM sign by the L side of the red brick offices. Exit via track which bears R, then immediately L into little wood, and over footbridge. Keep to the R side of field, and pass over stiles with stream to your R, to tarmac road.

Winchcombe

7. Cross drive to little gate and enter field, follow WM directions to gap in trees and WM post and stile. Over undulating field heading towards R of Copse, to bear half R around mound, down to R side of field to derelict farm behind stile. Over stile WM, follow track bearing R to Postlip Mills.

River Isbourne

Farm Buildings

Corndean Hall

Link to: Winchcombe

Wadfield Farm

Roman Villa

Newmeadow Farm

Disused Quarries

Humblebee Cottages

Disused Quarry

Hill Barn Farm

Stone Pillar

Belas Knap Long Barrow

Disused Quarry

6. From Belas Knap cross the stile and bear L through k/ gate. Follow WM sign with wood behind barbed wire fence on your R. Pass through next k/gate and descend along R side of field towards wood. Through k/gate and descend into wood to road. Turn L, follow road for 100 metres and as it swings R climb up steps to stile WM Postlip and enter field. Continue SA across field down to farm gate (wooden fence to your L) and over drive leading to Corndean Hall.

5. Through the gate onto farm track SP Cotswold Way with crumbling stone wall to your R. On reaching the derelict Wontley Farm bear L up rise and follow track SP Cotswold Way to stone pillar (entrance to Hill Barn Farm). Turn R SP Belas Knap along path with field to your R and thick hedge on your L to Belas Knap.

Undertake this bracing walk on a clear day and you will be richly rewarded with spectacular views of the Severn Valley, Malvern and Welsh Hills, Winchcombe and Sudeley Castle. From the Cotswolds highest viewpoint (1084ft/317metres) you cross Cleeve Common, an open space of moorland quality, along part of the Cotswold Way to a Stone Age Long Barrow, and onto a Jacobean Manor.

Distance
7 miles/11.2km. Short walk 1.5miles/2.4km.

Minimum Time
4 hours. Short walk 40 minutes.

Grade/Level of Difficulty
Easy/Moderate

Terrain/Paths
Springy turf, wide farm tracks

Landscape
Flat open moorland, undulating hills. Sheep pastures.

Dogs
Very popular dog walking area. Dogs can run free on Cleeve Common. Otherwise keep under control.

Public Toilets
Cleeve Hill

Parking (P)
Cleeve Hill P beside toilets or by golf club.

Recommended Start/ Finish
Cleeve Hill P

Location
On the B4632 between Cheltenham and Winchcombe.

CRANHAM WALK

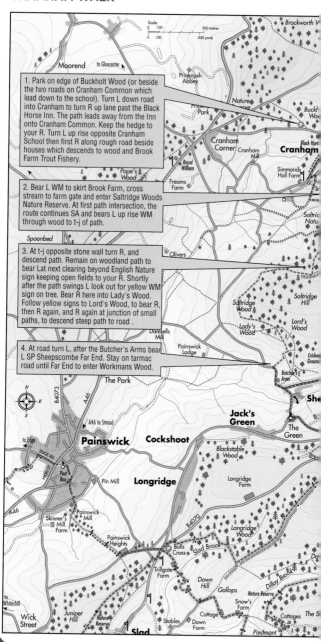

1. Park on edge of Buckholt Wood (or beside the two roads on Cranham Common which lead down to the school). Turn L down road into Cranham to turn R up lane past the Black Horse Inn. The path leads away from the Inn onto Cranham Common. Keep the hedge to your R. Turn L up rise opposite Cranham School then first R along rough road beside houses which descends to wood and Brook Farm Trout Fishery.

2. Bear L WM to skirt Brook Farm, cross stream to farm gate and enter Saltridge Woods Nature Reserve. At first path intersection, the route continues SA and bears L up rise WM through wood to t-j of path.

3. At t-j opposite stone wall turn R, and descend path. Remain on woodland path to bear L at next clearing beyond English Nature sign keeping open fields to your R. Shortly after the path swings L look out for yellow WM sign on tree. Bear R here into Lady's Wood. Follow yellow signs to Lord's Wood, to bear R, then R again, and R again at junction of small paths, to descend steep path to road .

4. At road turn L, after the Butcher's Arms bear L SP Sheepscombe Far End. Stay on tarmac road until Far End to enter Workmans Wood.

This could be described as a pub crawl, for the walk passes close to three popular inns, all with a reputation for good food. However, it also joins two delightful Cotswold villages affording wonderful views across a Cotswold landscape. Especially delightful are the trees in Saltridge Wood and the wildlife and flowers in the Nature Reserve. Best in early summer and autumn.

Distance
6 miles/9km.

Minimum Time
3 hours

Grade/Level of Difficulty
Easy/Moderate

Terrain/Paths
Woodland tracks, mud.

Landscape
Woodland, rolling pastureland, limestone villages.

Dogs
Keep under control in villages and on farm track/tarmac road. Lots of woodland where dogs can run free.

Public Toilets
None

Parking (P)
Buckholt Wood, Cranham.

Recommended Start/ Finish
Cranham

Location
Cranham and Sheepscombe are just off the B4070 between Stroud and Birdlip.

Map labels:

7. Follow road past Overtown Farm House ignoring first footpath sign. Shortly after Bramble Cottage turn R and enter Cranham Wood. Down steep bank to meet muddy woodland track. Follow the WM yellow/orange signs all the way to Cranham.

West Tump
Buckle Wood
Cranham Wood
B4070 to Birdlip
Nature reserve
Office
Bramble Cottage
Overtown Farm House
Overtown Farm
to Brimpsfield
Tumuli
Ebworth Farm
Ebworth House
National Trust Information Hut
Foston's Ash Inn
B4070
Wateredge Farm

6. Turn L at road and walk through trees, and L beyond driveway leading to Ebworth Estate, strike diagonally across field towards farm and TY mast. Bear L at road.

Hazle Manor
to Wishanger
Bunnage
Famish Hill Plantation
to Bisley
The Camp
Long Barrow

5. Follow the bridleway signs (blue arrows). On reaching the junction of paths opposite pond bear L, and SA on WM. Pass National Trust Information Hut. Keep following the blue arrows. Exit wood through farm gates to road.

High Wood

EASTLEACH WALK

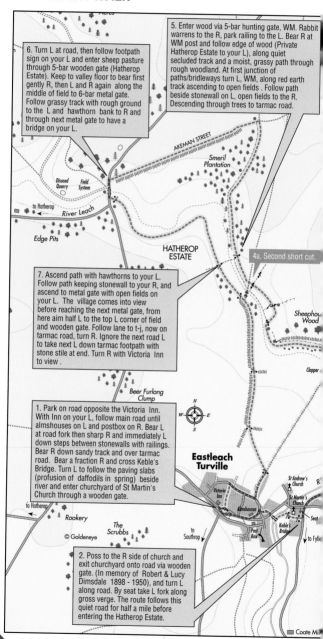

5. Enter wood via 5-bar hunting gate, WM. Rabbit warrens to the R, park railing to the L. Bear R at WM post and follow edge of wood (Private Hatherop Estate to your L), along quiet secluded track and a moist, grassy path through rough woodland. At first junction of paths/bridleways turn L, WM, along red earth track ascending to open fields . Follow path beside stonewall on L, open fields to the R. Descending through trees to tarmac road.

6. Turn L at road, then follow footpath sign on your L and enter sheep pasture through 5-bar wooden gate (Hatherop Estate). Keep to valley floor to bear first gently R, then L and R again along the middle of field to 6-bar metal gate. Follow grassy track with rough ground to the L and hawthorn bank to R and through next metal gate to have a bridge on your L.

Acres

AKEMAN STREET

Smeril Plantation

Disused Quarry *Field System*

to Hatherop *River Leach*

Edge Pits

HATHEROP ESTATE

4a. Second short cut.

Sheephou Wood

7. Ascend path with hawthorns to your L. Follow path keeping stonewall to your R, and ascend to metal gate with open fields on your L. The village comes into view before reaching the next metal gate, from here aim half L to the top L corner of field and wooden gate. Follow lane to t-j, now on tarmac road, turn R. Ignore the next road L to take next L down tarmac footpath with stone stile at end. Turn R with Victoria Inn to view .

Clapper

Beer Furlong Clump

N
W—E
S

1. Park on road opposite the Victoria Inn. With Inn on your L, follow main road until almshouses on L and postbox on R. Bear L at road fork then sharp R and immediately L down steps between stonewalls with railings. Bear R down sandy track and over tarmac road. Bear a fraction R and cross Keble's Bridge. Turn L to follow the paving slabs (profusion of daffodils in spring) beside river and enter churchyard of St Martin's Church through a wooden gate.

Eastleach Turville

St Andrew's Church
St Martin's Church
Seat

to Hotherop

Rookery

The Scrubs

© Goldeneye

to Southrop

Victoria Inn
Almshouses
Keble's Bridge
Post Box
to Fyfie

2. Poss to the R side of church and exit churchyard onto road via wooden gate. (In memory of Robert & Lucy Dimsdale 1898 - 1950), and turn L along road. By seat take L fork along gross verge. The route follows this quiet road for half a mile before entering the Hatherop Estate.

Coate Mill

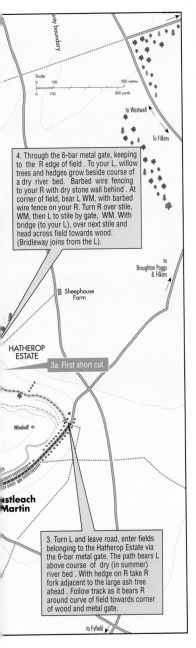

This walk starts from a traditional country inn noted for its rustic ales, and set in one of a pair of exquisite Cotswold villages situated on opposing banks of the River Leach. The route enters the Hatherop Estate and heads towards the upper reaches of the River Leach which in summer disappears underground, and crosses rolling sheep pastures beside stone walls - the quintessential Cotswold landscape.

Distance
4.5 miles/7.2km.

Minimum Time
2.5 hours

Grade/Level of Difficulty
Easy

Terrain/Paths
Tarmac, grassland, mud.

Landscape
Dry river valley, rolling sheep pastures.

Dogs
To be kept under control - beware livestock.

Public Toilets
None

Parking (P)
Opposite Victoria Inn

Recommended Start/ Finish
Eastleach Turville

Location
In between Burford, Lechlade and Fairford with access via the A417, and from the A361, turning opposite Filkins.

Text within the map image:

County boundary

Scale
0   100   500 metres
0   100   500 yards

to Westwell

To Filkins

4. Through the 6-bar metal gate, keeping to the R edge of field . To your L, willow trees and hedges grow beside course of a dry river bed. Barbed wire fencing to your R with dry stone wall behind . At corner of field, bear L WM, with barbed wire fence on your R. Turn R over stile, WM, then L to stile by gate, WM. With bridge (to your L), over next stile and head across field towards wood. (Bridleway joins from the L).

to Broughton Poggs & Filkins

Sheephouse Farm

HATHEROP ESTATE

3a. First short cut.

Windmill

Eastleach Martin

3. Turn L and leave road, enter fields belonging to the Hatherop Estate via the 6-bar metal gate. The path bears L above course of dry (in summer) river bed . With hedge on R take R fork adjacent to the large ash tree ahead . Follow track as it bears R around curve of field towards corner of wood and metal gate.

to Fyfield

GREAT TEW WALK

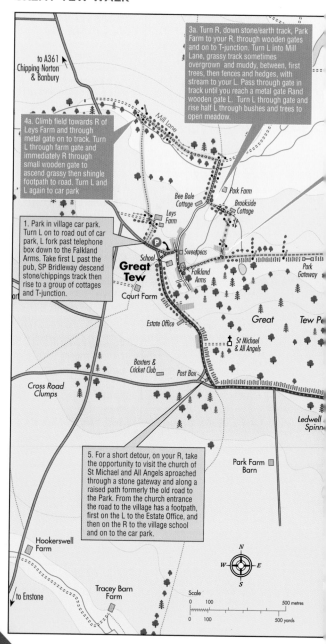

3a. Turn R, down stone/earth track, Park Farm to your R, through wooden gates and on to T-junction. Turn L into Mill Lane, grassy track sometimes overgrown and muddy, between, first trees, then fences and hedges, with stream to your L. Pass through gate in track until you reach a metal gate R and wooden gate L. Turn L through gate and rise half L through bushes and trees to open meadow.

4a. Climb field towards R of Leys Farm and through metal gate on to track. Turn L through farm gate and immediately R through small wooden gate to ascend grassy then shingle footpath to road. Turn L and L again to car park

1. Park in village car park. Turn L on to road out of car park, L fork past telephone box down to the Falkland Arms. Take first L past the pub, SP Bridleway descend stone/chippings track then rise to a group of cottages and T-junction.

5. For a short detour, on your R, take the opportunity to visit the church of St Michael and All Angels approached through a stone gateway and along a raised path formerly the old road to the Park. From the church entrance the road to the village has a footpath, first on the L to the Estate Office, and then on the R to the village school and on to the car park.

to A361
Chipping Norton
& Banbury

Mill Lane

Park Farm

Bee Bole
Cottage

Brookside
Cottage

Leys
Farm

Sweetpeas

School

Great
Tew

Falkland
Arms

Park
Gateway

Court Farm

Estate Office

Great

Tew Pe

St Michael
& All Angels

Baxters &
Cricket Club

Post Box

Cross Road
Clumps

Ledwell
Spinn

Park Farm
Barn

Hookerswell
Farm

to Enstone

Tracey Barn
Farm

Scale

0   100   500 metres

0   100   500 yards

N
W   E
S

The first, short walk takes you around the village past idyllic cottage gardens surmounted by thatched or roof tiles and down to an overgrown spinney. The second walk circumnavigates the Great Park, a C19 Arboretum planted by John Claudius Loudon. Bring your book on trees!

Distance
Walk 1: 1.5 miles/2.4km.
Walk 2: 2.5 miles/4km

Minimum Time
Walk 1: 1 hour.
Walk 2: 1.5 hours.

Grade/Level of Difficulty
Easy

Terrain/Paths
Tracks, mud, grass.

Landscape
Arable fields, woodland.

Dogs
To be kept under control at all times.

Public Toilets
None

Parking (P)
Great Tew village car park

Recommended Start/Finish
From P or in village.

Location
Situated between Banbury and Chipping Norton just off the A361 on the B4022 leading to Enstone and the A44.

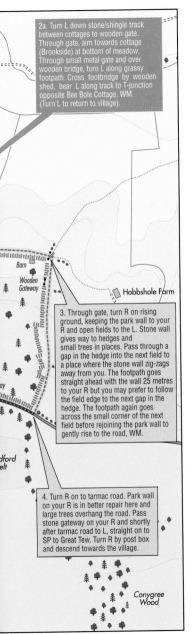

2a. Turn L down stone/shingle track between cottages to wooden gate. Through gate, aim towards cottage (Brookside) at bottom of meadow. Through small metal gate and over wooden bridge, turn L along grassy footpath. Cross footbridge by wooden shed, bear L along track to T-junction opposite Bee Bole Cottage, WM. (Turn L to return to village).

Barn

Wooden Gateway

Hobbshole Farm

3. Through gate, turn R on rising ground, keeping the park wall to your R and open fields to the L. Stone wall gives way to hedges and small trees in places. Pass through a gap in the hedge into the next field to a place where the stone wall zig-zags away from you. The footpath goes straight ahead with the wall 25 metres to your R but you may prefer to follow the field edge to the next gap in the hedge. The footpath again goes across the small corner of the next field before rejoining the park wall to gently rise to the road, WM.

dford elt

4. Turn R on to tarmac road. Park wall on your R is in better repair here and large trees overhang the road. Pass stone gateway on your R and shortly after tarmac road to L, straight on to SP to Great Tew. Turn R by post box and descend towards the village.

Conygree Wood

THE SLAUGHTERS WALK

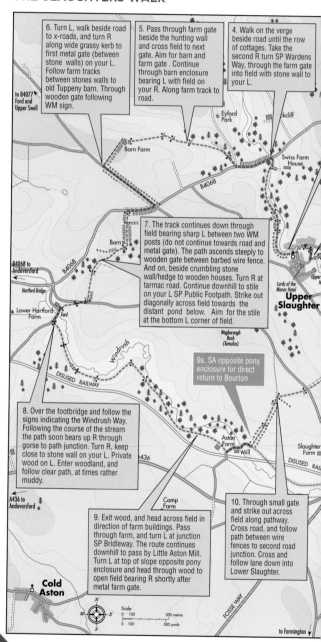

6. Turn L, walk beside road to x-roads, and turn R along wide grassy kerb to first metal gate (between stone walls) on your L. Follow farm tracks between stones walls to old Tuppeny barn. Through wooden gate following WM sign.

5. Pass through farm gate beside the hunting wall and cross field to next gate. Aim for barn and farm gate. Continue through barn enclosure bearing L with field on your R. Along farm track to road.

4. Walk on the verge beside road until the row of cottages. Take the second R turn SP Wardens Way, through the farm gate into field with stone wall to your L.

7. The track continues down through field bearing sharp L between two WM posts (do not continue towards road and metal gate). The path ascends steeply to wooden gate between barbed wire fence. And on, beside crumbling stone wall/hedge to wooden houses. Turn R to stile on tarmac road. Continue downhill to stile on your L SP Public Footpath. Strike out diagonally across field towards the distant pond below. Aim for the stile at the bottom L corner of field.

8. Over the footbridge and follow the signs indicating the Windrush Way. Following the course of the stream the path soon bears up R through gorse to path junction. Turn R, keep close to stone wall on your L. Private wood on L. Enter woodland, and follow clear path, at times rather muddy.

9a. SA opposite pony enclosure for direct return to Bourton

9. Exit wood, and head across field in direction of farm buildings. Pass through farm, and turn L at junction SP Bridleway. The route continues downhill to pass by Little Aston Mill. Turn L at top of slope opposite pony enclosure and head through wood to open field bearing R shortly after metal farm gate.

10. Through small gate and strike out across field along pathway. Cross road, and follow path between wire fences to second road junction. Cross and follow lane down into Lower Slaughter.

to B4077 Ford and Upper Swell

Eyford Park

ckcliff

Swiss Farm House

Barn Farm

B4068

Barn

B4068 to Andoversford

B4068

Hartford Bridge

Lower Hartford Farm

Ford

Windrush

DISUSED RAILWAY

A436 to Andoversford

436

Camp Farm

Cold Aston

Lords of the Manor Hotel

Upper

Upper Slaughter

Wagborough Bush (Tumulus)

Aston Farm

Mill

Slaughter Farm

DISUSED RAI

FOSSE WAY

to Farmington

N
W E
S

Scale
0 100   500 metres
0 100   500 yards

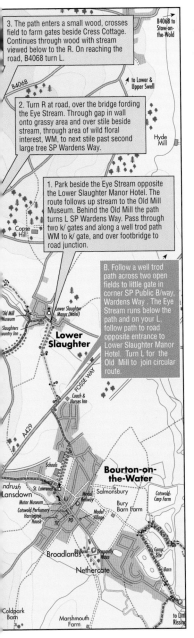

3. The path enters a small wood, crosses field to farm gates beside Cress Cottage. Continues through wood with stream viewed below to the R. On reaching the road, B4068 turn L.

2. Turn R at road, over the bridge fording the Eye Stream. Through gap in wall onto grassy area and over stile beside stream, through area of wild floral interest, WM, to next stile past second large tree SP Wardens Way.

1. Park beside the Eye Stream opposite the Lower Slaughter Manor Hotel. The route follows up stream to the Old Mill Museum. Behind the Old Mill the path turns L SP Wardens Way. Pass through two k/ gates and along a well trod path WM to k/ gate, and over footbridge to road junction.

B. Follow a well trod path across two open fields to little gate in corner SP Public B/way, Wardens Way . The Eye Stream runs below the path and on your L, follow path to road opposite entrance to Lower Slaughter Manor Hotel. Turn L for the Old Mill to join circular route.

A good half days walk that joins two of the Cotswolds most famous villages known jointly as The Slaughters. Home to Cotswold stone cottages and beautifully tended gardens and some enchanting Country House hotels. The route enters, for many, unknown territory and follows the upper reaches of the Eye Stream and River Windrush. It cuts through a rich meadow of wild flowers beside the Eye Stream and crosses undulating farmland and picturesque woodland.

Distance
7.25 miles/11.6km

Minimum Time
4 hours

Grade/Level of Difficulty
Moderate

Terrain/Paths
Muddy paths, springy turf, farm track.

Landscape
River valleys, rolling farmland, woodland.

Dogs
Keep under control across farmland. Despite some sections along roadside grass verges, this walk is away from the crowds so quite good for dogs.

Public Toilets
None

Parking (P)
Beside Eye Stream, Lower Slaughter, or outside church at Upper Slaughter.

Recommended Start/Finish
Lower or Upper Slaughter P.

Location
Just off the A429 between Bourton and Stow

WINCHCOMBE WALK

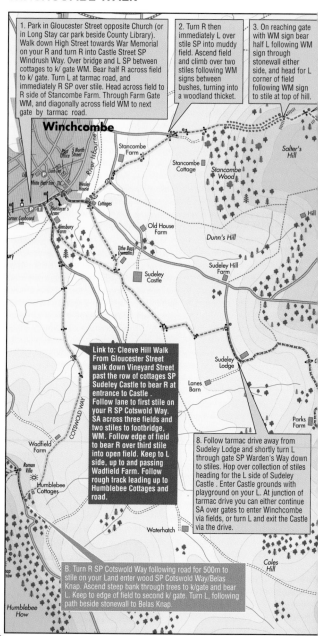

1. Park in Gloucester Street opposite Church (or in Long Stay car park beside County Library). Walk down High Street towards War Memorial on your R and turn R into Castle Street SP Windrush Way. Over bridge and L SP between cottages to k/ gate WM. Bear half R across field to k/ gate. Turn L at tarmac road, and immediately R SP over stile. Head across field to R side of Stancombe Farm. Through Farm Gate WM, and diagonally across field WM to next gate by tarmac road.

2. Turn R then immediately L over stile SP into muddy field. Ascend field and climb over two stiles following WM signs between bushes, turning into a woodland thicket.

3. On reaching gate with WM sign bear half L following WM sign through stonewall either side, and head for L corner of field following WM sign to stile at top of hill.

Winchcombe

Post Office 5 North Street

Lion Inn

Library

White Hart Inn TIC

Wesley House

Plaisterer's Arms

Cottages

Corner Cupboard Inn

Almsbury Farm

Tithe Barn (remains)

Sudeley Castle

Stancombe Farm

Stancombe Cottage

Stancombe Wood

Old House Farm

Dunn's Hill

Sudeley Hill Farm

Salter's Hill

Hill

Sudeley Lodge

Lanes Barn

Parks Farm

COTSWOLD WAY

Wadfield Farm

Roman Villa

Humblebee Cottages

Waterhatch

Coles Hill

Humblebee How

Link to: Cleeve Hill Walk
From Gloucester Street walk down Vineyard Street past the row of cottages SP Sudeley Castle to bear R at entrance to Castle .
Follow lane to first stile on your R SP Cotswold Way. SA across three fields and two stiles to footbridge, WM. Follow edge of field to bear R over third stile into open field. Keep to L side, up to and passing Wadfield Farm. Follow rough track leading up to Humblebee Cottages and road.

8. Follow tarmac drive away from Sudeley Lodge and shortly turn L through gate SP Warden's Way down to stiles. Hop over collection of stiles heading for the L side of Sudeley Castle . Enter Castle grounds with playground on your L. At junction of tarmac drive you can either continue SA over gates to enter Winchcombe via fields, or turn L and exit the Castle via the drive.

B. Turn R SP Cotswold Way following road for 500m to stile on your L and enter wood SP Cotswold Way/Belas Knap. Ascend steep bank through trees to k/gate and bear L. Keep to edge of field to second k/ gate. Turn L, following path beside stonewall to Belas Knap.

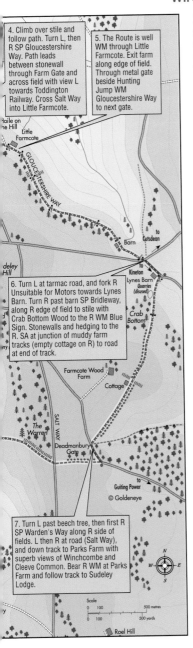

4. Climb over stile and follow path. Turn L, then R SP Gloucestershire Way. Path leads between stonewall through Farm Gate and across field with view L towards Toddington Railway. Cross Salt Way into Little Farmcote.

5. The Route is well WM through Little Farmcote. Exit farm along edge of field. Through metal gate beside Hunting Jump WM Gloucestershire Way to next gate.

6. Turn L at tarmac road, and fork R Unsuitable for Motors towards Lynes Barn. Turn R past barn SP Bridleway, along R edge of field to stile with Crab Bottom Wood to the R WM Blue Sign. Stonewalls and hedging to the R. SA at junction of muddy farm tracks (empty cottage on R) to road at end of track.

7. Turn L past beech tree, then first R SP Warden's Way along R side of fields. L then R at road (Salt Way), and down track to Parks Farm with superb views of Winchcombe and Cleeve Common. Bear R WM at Parks Farm and follow track to Sudeley Lodge.

© Goldeneye

It is worth a wander around the historic village of Winchcombe before the climb up Salters Hill. At first this is a fairly energetic ascent, thereafter the route is comparatively easy. The views north towards the Vale of Evesham are a delight. And as you cross the Salt Way and bear down on Parks Farm the views towards Cleeve Common and left up the valley are magnificent. Return to Winchcombe through the parkland of Sudeley Castle.

Distance
10 miles / 16km

Minimum Time
4 hours

Grade / Level of Difficulty
Moderate

Terrain / Paths
Stone paths, farm tracks, grass.

Landscape
Patchwork of arable fields, sheep pastures, rolling hills, woodland.

Dogs
Quite a lot of farm tracks through sheep pastures. Keep under control at all times.

Public Toilets
Winchcombe High Street

Parking
Gloucester Street opposite Church, or in Long Stay beside County Library.

Recommended Start / Finish
Winchcombe High Street

Location
Midway between Cheltenham and Broadway on the B4632.

83

MAPS OF THE COTSWOLDS: LEGEND

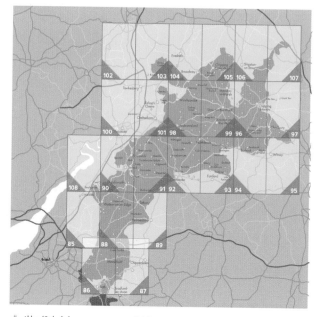

♙ Abbey/Cathedral	⚑ Pub/Inn	⊕ Leisure/Sports Centre
✕ Battle Site	⚑ Railway Interest	⚓ Lifeboat
⚶ Bed & Breakfast Accomodation	✕ Restaurant	℗ Parking
☕ Café	⚑ Self Catering Accommodation	⊼ Picnic Site
⚏ Castle	⊓ Standing Stone/Barrow	⚐⚑ Tents & Caravans
⚑ Church/Chapel of Interest	♨ Theatre/Concert Hall	△ Sailing
⚏ Cinema	ℹ Tourist Information	⚓ Surfing
⚑ Craft Interest	⚶ Tumulus/Tumuli	ℹ Tourist Information
♱ Cross	☀ Viewpoint	⚓ Windsurfing
⚙ Cycleway	✳ Windmill/Wind Farm	▲ Youth Hostel
⊕ Fun Park/Leisure Park	⊕ Airfield	⚶ Agricultural Interest
✳ Hill Fort/Ancient Settlement	⚓ Boat Trips	⚶ Arboretum
⚏ Historic Building	⚓ Aquarium	⚶ Bird Reserve
⚏ Hotel	⚑ Camping Site (Tents)	✿ Garden of Interest
⚏ Industrial Interest	⚑ Caravan Site	⚶ Vineyard
⚗ Karting	⚶⚶ Ferry (Pedestrians)	⚑ Walks/Nature Trails
⚏ Lighthouse	⚓ Ferry (Vehicles)	✦ Wildlife Park
⚏ Mining Interest/Engine Houses	⚓ Fishing Trips	⚓ Zoo
☆ Miscellaneous/Natural Attraction	⚑ 9/18 Hole Golf Course	∪ Horse Riding
⚏ Museum/Art Gallery	⚓ Harbour	℗ National Trust Car Park
⚱ Pottery	⚓ Inshore Rescue Boat	

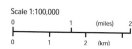

A Road

B Road

Minor Road

Other Road or Track
(not necessarily with public
or vehicular access)

Railway

Cycleway

381m.
305m.
229m.
152m
76m.

Open Space owned
by the National Trust

Built-up Area

Scale 1:100,000

| 0 | 1 | (miles) | 2 |

| 0 | 1 | 2 | (km) |

84

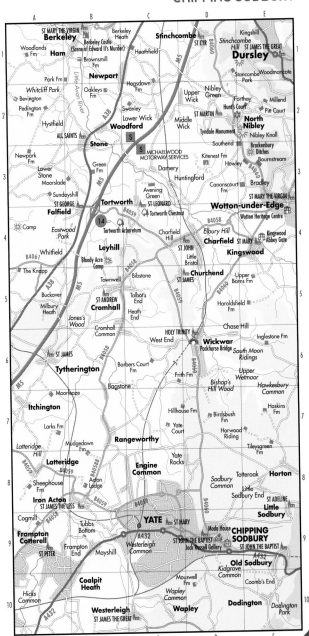

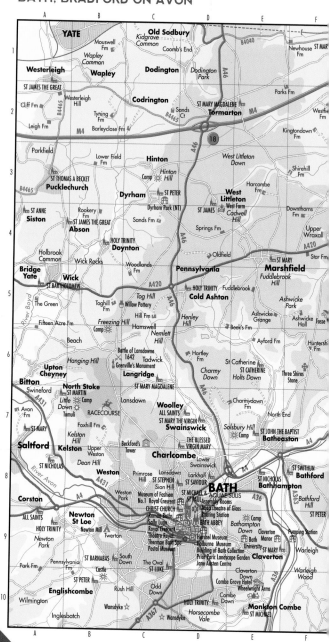

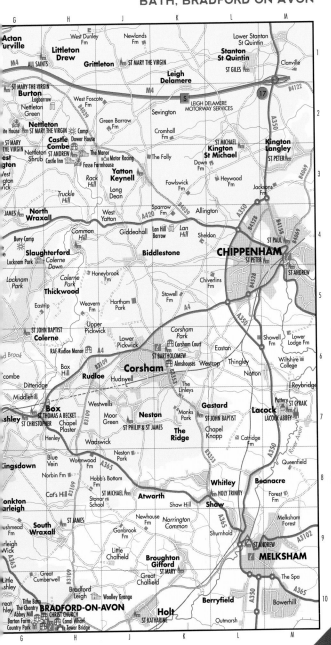

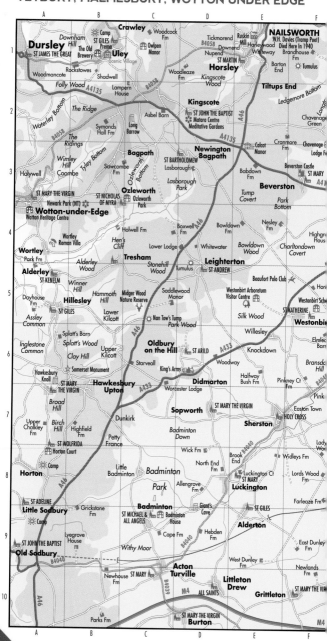

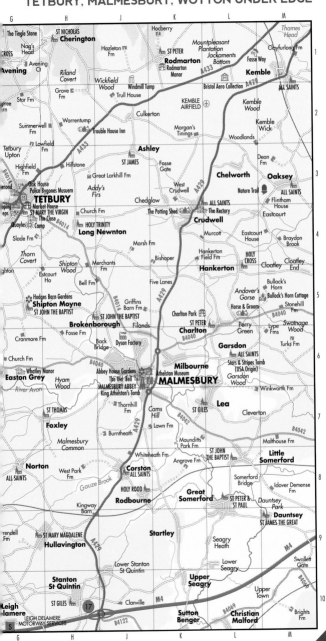

The Tingle Stone
ST NICHOLAS **Cherington**
Hocberry
Nag's Head
Avening
CROSS

Mountpleasant
Plantation
Jackaments
Bottom
Fosse Way
Clayfurlong Fm
Thames Head

ST PETER **Rodmarton**
Rodmarton Manor
Hazleton Fm

Riland Covert
Wickfield Wood
Windmill Tump
Trull House

Bristol Aero Collection **Kemble**
ALL SAINTS

Grove Fm
Star Fm

KEMBLE AIRFIELD
Kemble Wood
Kemble Wick

Warrentump
Trouble House Inn
Culkerton

Woodlands

Summerwell Fm
Lowfield Fm

Morgan's Tinings

Tetbury Upton
Highfield Fm
Hillstone
Ashley
ST JAMES
Fosse Gate

Dean Fm

Chelworth
Oaksey
ALL SAINTS
Flintham House

Oak House
Police Bygones Museum
TETBURY
Market House
ST MARY THE VIRGIN
The Close
Quayles Camp

Great Larkhill Fm
Addy's Firs

West Crudwell

Nature Trail

Eastcourt

Chedglow
ALL SAINTS
The Potting Shed
The Rectory
Crudwell

Slade Fm
Church Fm
HOLY TRINITY
Long Newnton

Marsh Fm

Murcott
Eastcourt House

Braydon Brook

Thorn Covert
Shipton Wood
Merchants Fm
Bishoper
Hankerton Field Fm
HOLY CROSS
Cloatley
Cloatley End

Estcourt Ho
Bell Fm
Five Lanes
Hankerton

Bullock's Horn
Andover's Gorse
Bullock's Horn Cottage
Stonehill Fm

Hodges Barn Gardens
Shipton Moyne
ST JOHN THE BAPTIST
Griffins Barn Fm
Charlton Park
ST PETER
Horse & Groom
B4040
Lype Fms
Swatnage Wood

Brokenborough
Filands
Charlton
B4040
Perry Green
Turks Fm

Cranmore Fm
Fosse Fm
Back Bridge
Dyson Factory

Garsdon
ALL SAINTS
Stars & Stripes Tomb (USA Origin)

Church Fm
B4040
Abbey House Gardens
Athelston Museum
Milbourne
Garsdon Wood

Whatley Manor
Easton Grey
Hyam Wood
The Old Bell
MALMESBURY ABBEY
MALMESBURY
King Athelstan's Tomb
Winkworth Fm

River Avon

ST THOMAS
Thornhill
Cams Hill
ST GILES
Lea
Cleverton
B4042

Foxley
Burntheath
Lawn Fm
Maunditts Park Fm

Malmesbury Common
Whiteheath Fm
Angrove Fm
ST JOHN THE BAPTIST
Little Somerford

Norton
ALL SAINTS
West Park Fm
Corston
ALL SAINTS
Somerford Bridge
Idover Demense Fm

Gauze Brook
HOLY ROOD
Great Somerford
ST PETER & ST PAUL
Dauntsey Park
Dauntsey
ST JAMES THE GREAT

Kingway Barn
Rodbourne

rendell Fm
ST MARY MAGDALENE
Hullavington
Startley
Seagry Heath
Swallett Gate
M4

Stanton St Quintin
ST GILES
17
Lower Stanton St Quintin
Clanville
M4
Lower Seagry
Upper Seagry
Upper Town

Leigh Delamere
LEIGH DELAMERE MOTORWAY SERVICES
S
B4122
Sutton Benger
B4069
Christian Malford
Brights Fm

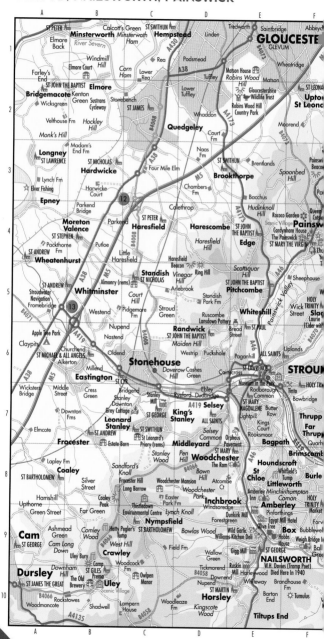

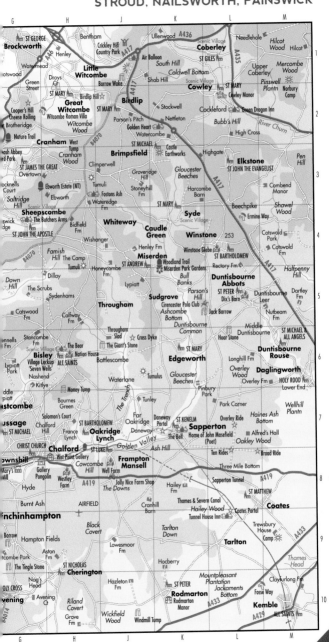

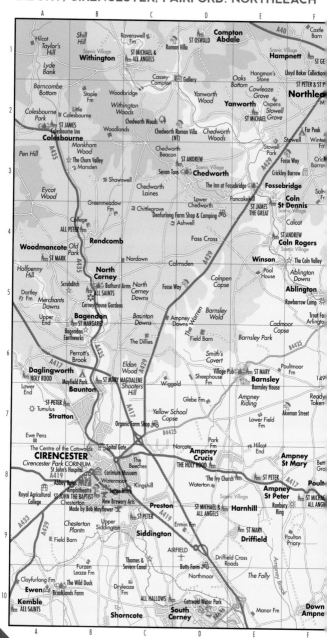

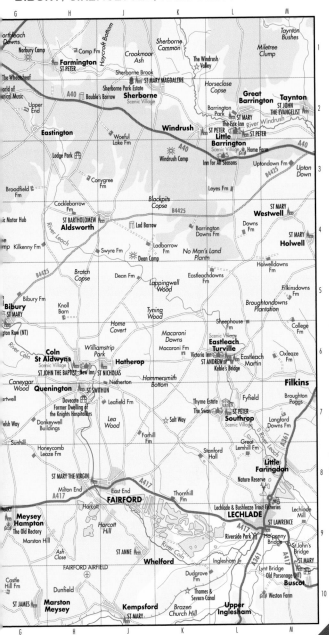

orthleach Downs

Norbury Camp

Camp Inn

Hoycroft Bottom

Crookmoor Ash

Sherborne Common

The Windrush Valley

Taynton Bushes

Miletree Clump

Farmington
ST PETER

The Wheatsheaf

orld of nical Music

A40

Bauble's Barrow

Sherborne Park Estate

Sherborne Brook

ST MARY MAGDALENE

Sherborne
Scenic Village

Horseclose Copse

Great Barrington
ST MARY

Taynton
ST JOHN
THE EVANGELIST

Upper End

Barrington Park

ST MARY

River Windrush

Eastington

Woeful Lake Fm

Windrush
ST PETER

A40

The Fox Inn

Little Barrington
Scenic Village

ST PETER

Home Farm

A40

Lodge Park

A40

Windrush Camp

Inn for All Seasons

Uptodown Fm

B4425

Upton Down

Broadfield Fm

Cocklebarrow Fm

Blackpits Copse

B4425

Leyes Fm

Westwell
ST MARY

ic Motor Hub

ST BARTHOLOMEW

Aldsworth

Lad Barrow

Barrington Downs Fm

Downs Fm

ST MARY
Holwell

mp Kilkenny Fm

River Leach

Swyre Fm

Ladbarrow Fm

Dean Camp

No Man's Land Plantn

Holwelldowns Fm

B4425

Bratch Copse

Dean Fm

Lappingwell Wood

Eastleachdowns Fm

Broughtondowns Plantation

Filkinsdowns Fm

Bibury
ST MARY

Bibury Fm

Knoll Barn

Home Covert

Tyning Wood

Macaroni Downs

Sheephouse Fm

College Fm

ton Row (NT)

Williamstrip Park

Macaroni Fm

Scenic Village

Eastleach Turville
ST ANDREW

Victoria Inn

Eastleach Martin

Oxleaze Fm

River Coln

Coln St Aldwyns
Scenic Village

Hatherop
ST NICHOLAS

Hammersmith Bottom

Keble's Bridge

Coneygar Wood

ST JOHN THE BAPTIST

New Inn

Netherton

Filkins

artwell

Quenington
ST SWITHUN

Dovecote
Former Dwelling of the Knights Hospitallers

Leafield Fm

Thyme Estate

Fyfield

Broughton Poggs

elsh Way

Donkeywell Buildings

Lea Wood

Salt Way

The Swan

Southrop
Scenic Village

ST PETER

Langford Downs Fm

Sunhill

Honeycomb Leaze Fm

Farhill Fm

Great Lemhill Fm

River Leach

A361

ST MARY THE VIRGIN

Stanford Hall

Little Faringdon

Milton End

East End

A417

Thornhill Fm

Nature Reserve

MARY

A417

FAIRFORD

Horcott

Lechlade & Bushleaze Trout Fisheries

LECHLADE
ST LAWRENCE

Lechlade Mill

Meysey Hampton
The Old Rectory

Harcott Hill

Riverside Park

Ha'penny Bridge

St John's Bridge

Marston Hill

Ash Close

ST ANNE

River Coln

Inglesham

ST MARY

A361

A41

Castle Hill Fm

FAIRFORD AIRFIELD

Whelford

Dudgrove Fm

Lynt Bridge
Old Parsonage (HT)

Buscot

ST JAMES

Dunfield

Kempsford
ST MARY

Thames & Severn Canal

Brazen Church Hill

Upper Inglesham

Weston Farm

Marston Meysey

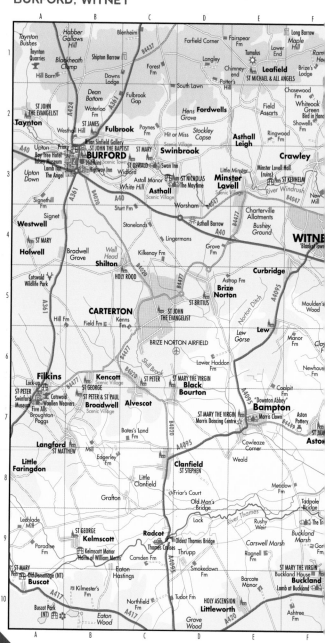

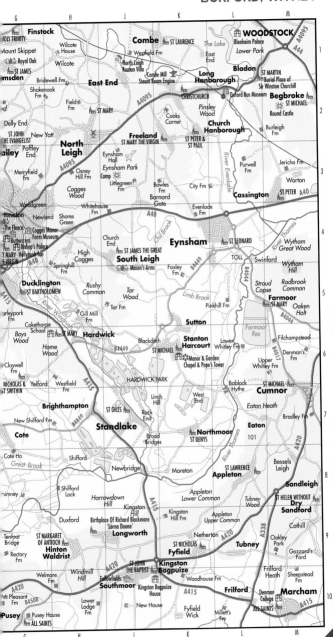

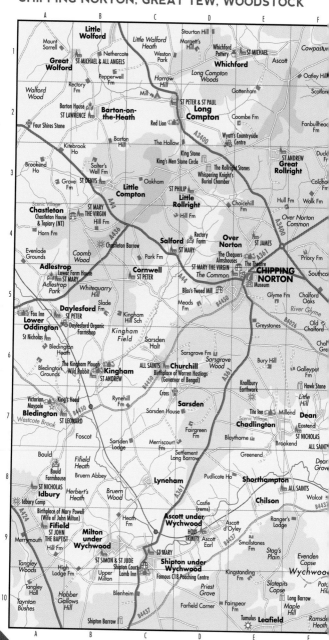

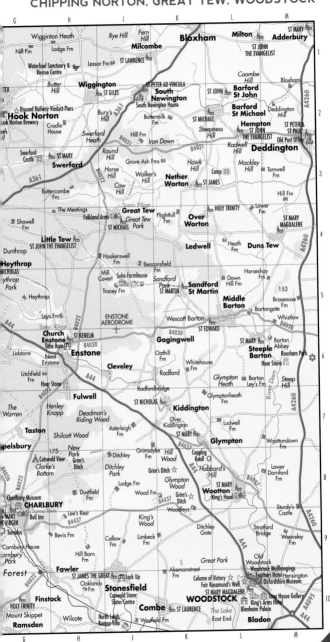

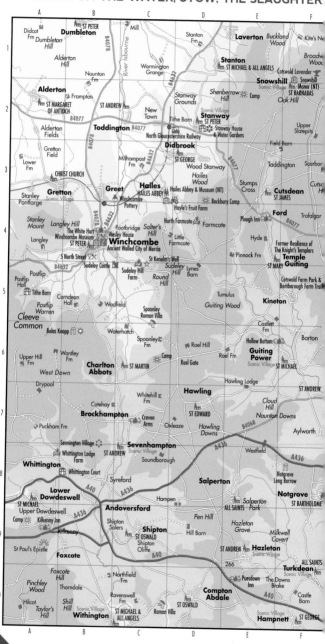

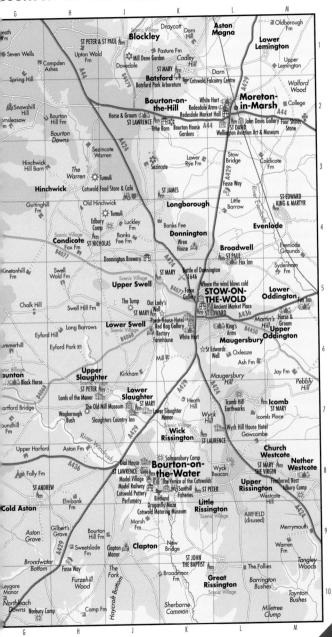

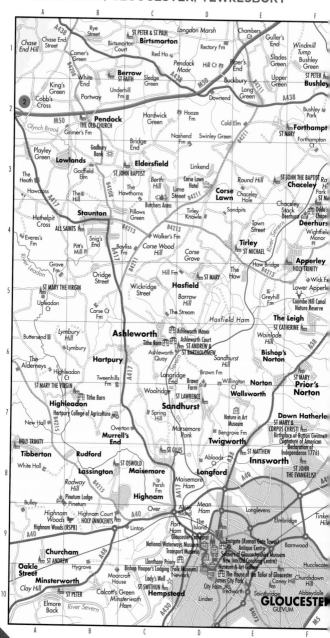

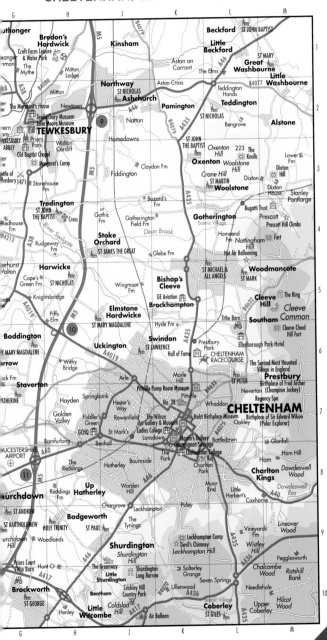

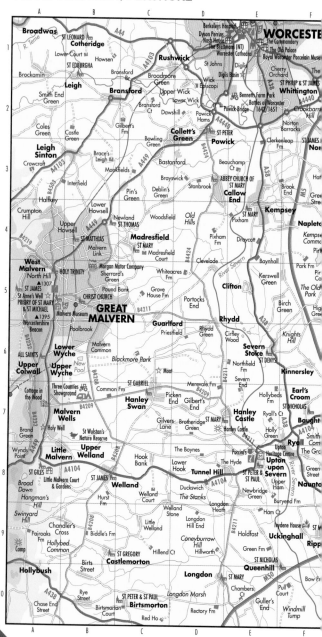

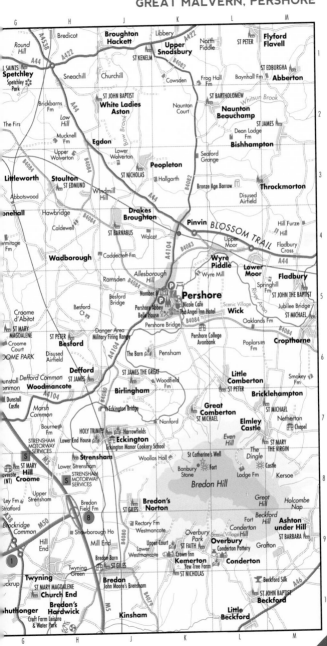

Round Hill
Bredicot
Libbery
North Piddle
ST PETER
Flyford Flavell

L SAINTS
Spetchley
Spetchley Park
Broughton Hackett
ST KENELM
Upper Snodsbury
ST EDBURGHA
Abberton

The Firs
Sneachill
Churchill
Cowsden
Frog Hall
Baynhall Fm
Whitsun Brook

Brickbarns Fm
Low Hill
ST JOHN BAPTIST
White Ladies Aston
ST BARTHOLOMEW
Naunton Court
Naunton Beauchamp
ST JAMES

Mucknell Fm
Egdon
Lower Wolverton
Dean Lodge Fm
Bishhampton

Upper Wolverton
Peopleton
Seaford Grange

Littleworth
Stoulton
ST EDMUND
ST NICHOLAS
Hallgarth
Bronze Age Barrow
Throckmorton

Abbotswood
Hawbridge
Windmill Hill
Disused Airfield

onehall
Caldewell
Drakes Broughton
Pinvin
BLOSSOM TRAIL
Hill Furze
Hill

ermitage Fm
ST BARNABUS
Walcot
Upper Moor
Fladbury Cross

Wadborough
Caddecroft Fm
A4104
B4083
Wyre Piddle
Lower Moor
A44
Fladbury

Allesborough Hill
Wyre Mill
Springhill
ST JOHN THE BAPTIST

Ramsden
Number 8
Pershore
Wick
Jubilee Bridge
ST MICHAEL

Croome d'Abitot
Besford Ct
Besford Bridge
Pershore Abbey
Nicole Café
Bella House
The Angel Inn Hotel
Scenic Village
Oaklands Fm

ST MARY MAGDALENE
ST PETER
Pershore Bridge
Pershore College Avonbank
Cropthorne

OOME PARK
Besford
Danger Area Military Firing Range
Poplars Fm

Croome Court
Disused Airfield
The Barn
Pensham

unstall ommon
Defford
ST JAMES
ST JAMES THE GREAT
Woodfield Fm
Little Comberton
ST PETER
Smokey Fm

Dunstall Castle
Woodmancote
Birlingham
Bricklehampton

Marsh Common
Nanford
Great Comberton
ST MICHAEL
ST MICHAEL

Bourne Fm
HOLY TRINITY
Harrowfields
Elmley Castle
Netherton
Chapel

Lower End House
Eckington
Eckington Manor Cookery School
Even Hill
The Dingle
ST MARY THE VIRGIN

STRENSHAM MOTORWAY SERVICES
Woollas Hall
St Catherine's Well
Castle
Kersoe

ST MARY Hill Croome (NT)
Strensham
Lower Strensham
Banbury Stone
Fort
Lodge Fm

avocote
STRENSHAM MOTORWAY SERVICES
Bredon Hill
Great Hill
Holcombe Nap

Ley Fm
Upper Strensham
Bredon Field Fm
ST GILES
Bredon's Norton
Fort
Beckford Hill
Ashton under Hill

Stratford
Showborough Ho
Rectory Fm
Westmancote
Overbury Park
Scenic Village Hill
ST BARBARA

Brockridge Common
Mill End
Upper Court
Lower Westmancote
ST FAITH
Overbury
Conderton Pottery
Grafton

Hill End
Bredon Barn
Crown Inn
Kemerton
Yew Tree Farm
Conderton

uckrup
Twyning
Twyning Green
ST NICHOLAS
Beckford Silk

ST MARY MAGDALENE
Church End
Bredon
John Moore's Brensham
ST JOHN BAPTIST
Beckford

huttonger
Bredon's Hardwick
Kinsham
Little Beckford

Croft Farm Leisure & Water Park

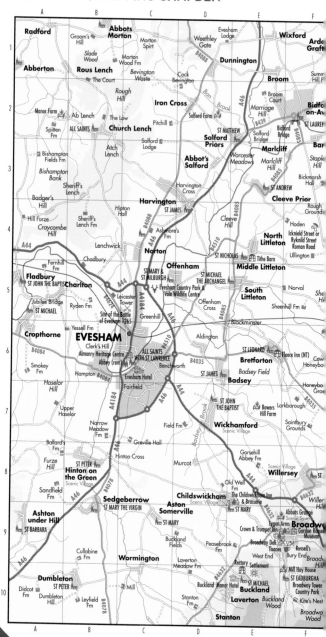

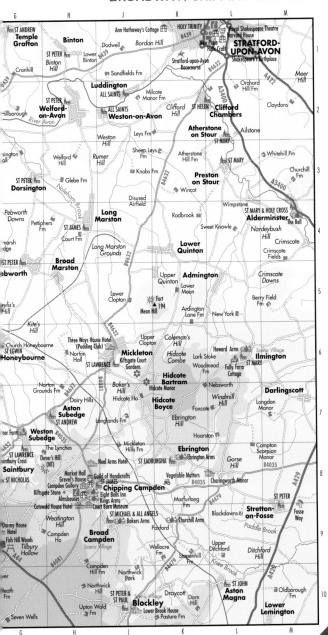

ST ANDREW
Temple Grafton
Binton
ST PETER
Lower Binton
Binton Hill
Dodwell
Bordon Hill
B439
HOLY TRINITY
New Place Hall's Croft
Royal Shakespeare Theatre
Harvard House
STRATFORD-UPON-AVON
Shakespeare's Birthplace

Cranhill
Sandfields Fm
Stratford-upon-Avon Racecourse
B4632
Meer Hill

Luddington
ALL SAINTS
Milcote Manor Fm
Orchard Hill Fm
A422

ST PETER
Welford-on-Avon
ALL SAINTS
Weston-on-Avon
Clifford Hill
ST HELEN
Clifford Chambers
Claydons

Hillborough
River Avon
Weston Hill
Leys Fm
Atherstone on Stour
ST MARY
Ailstone
Whitehill Fm

sington all
Welford Hill
Rumer Hill
Sheep Leys Fm
Atherstone Hill Fm
ST MARY
Churchill Fm
A3400

ST PETER
Dorsington
Glebe Fm
Noleham Brook
Knobs Fm
B4632
Preston on Stour
Wimpstone
ST MARY & HOLY CROSS
Alderminster
The Bell

Pebworth Downs
Pettiphers Fm
Long Marston
Disused Airfield
Wincot
Radbrook
Sweet Knowle
Nardeybush Fm
Crimscote

marsh dge
ST PETER
ST JAMES
Court Fm
Long Marston Grounds
B4632
Lower Quinton
Crimscote Fields

ebworth
Broad Marston
Lower Clopton
Upper Quinton
Lower Meon
Admington
Crimscote Downs

ylis's Hill
Kite's Hill
Fort 194
Meon Hill
Ardington Lane Fm
New York
Berry Field Fm

Church Honeybourne
Honeybourne
Three Ways House Hotel (Pudding Club)
Norton Hall
Upper Clopton
Coleman's Hill
Howard Arms
Lark Stoke
Scenic Village
ST MARY
Ilmington

Norton Grounds Fm
B4081
ST LAWRENCE
Mickleton
Kiftsgate Court Gardens
Hidcote Combe
Woodmead Fm
Folly Farm Cottage

Dairy Hills
Baker's Hill
Hidcote Bartrim
Hidcote Manor
Nebsworth
Darlingscott

Aston Subedge
ST ANDREW
Longlands Fm
Hidcote Ho
Hidcote Boyce
Windmill Fm
Foxcote
Longdon Manor

nor Farm
Weston Subedge
ST EGWIN
The Lynches
Mickleton Hills Fm
Ebrington Hill
Hoarston

ntbury Cross
Saintbury
ST LAWRENCE
Dover's Hill (NT)
Noel Arms Hotel
ST EADBURGHA
Ebrington
Ebrington Arms
Gorse Hill
Campton Scorpion Manor
B4035

ST NICHOLAS
Market Hall
Grevel's House
Guild of Handicrafts
ST JAMES
Vegetable Matters
B4035
Charingworth Manor
A429
ST PETER

Kiftsgate Stone
Campden Gallery
Almshouses
Cotswold House Hotel
Chipping Campden
Eight Bells Inn
Kings Arms
Court Barn Museum
Marfurlong Fm
B4479
Blackdowns
Stretton-on-Fosse
Fosse Way

Dormy House Hotel
Weatington Hill
Campden Ho
ST MICHAEL & ALL ANGELS
Bakers Arms
Churchill Arms
Paxford

Fish Hill Woods
Tilbury Hollow
Broad Campden
Scenic Village
Wellacre
Stapenhill Fm
Upper Ditchford
Ditchford Hill

A44
Camden Hill Fm
Northwick Park
B4479
Knee Brook
Paddle Brook

eath
Seven Wells
Northwick Fm
ST PETER & ST PAUL
Scenic Village
Upton Wold Fm
Blockley
Lower Brook House
Pasture Fm
Draycott
Dorn Hill
ST JOHN
Aston Magna
Oldborough Fm
Lower Lemington

105

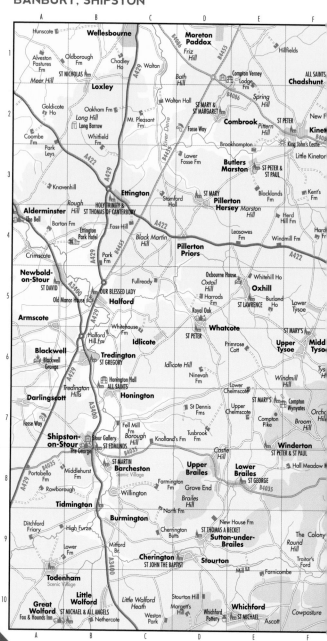

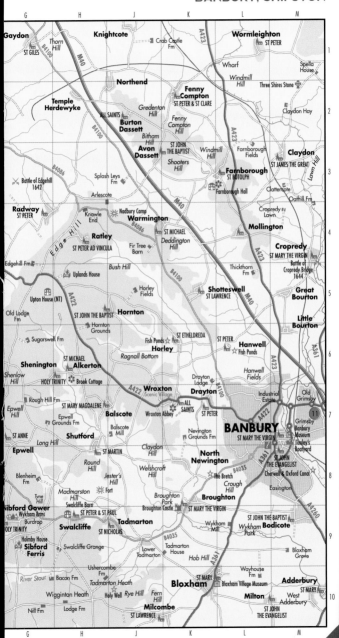

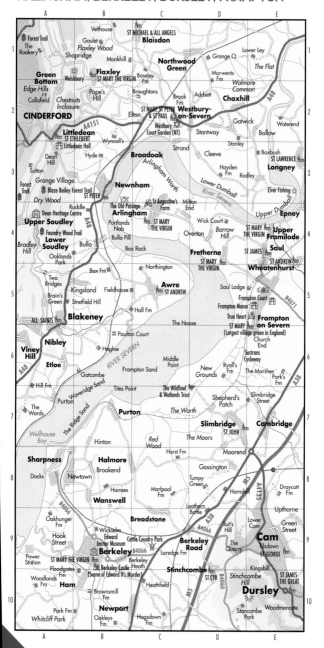

INDEX TO FEATURED ATTRACTIONS

Laburnam Walk, Barnsley House

INDEX TO FEATURED ATTRACTIONS

INDEX TO FEATURED ATTRACTIONS

INDEX TO FEATURED ATTRACTIONS